W9-CFG-180

The Commonsense MBA

The Seven Practices of Enduring Businesses for the Entrepreneur

The Commonsense MBA

The Seven Practices of Enduring Businesses for the Entrepreneur

by Richard M. Astle

St. Martin's Griffin
New York

THE COMMONSENSE MBA. Copyright © 1994 by Richard M. Astle. All rights reserved. Printed in the United States of America. No part of this book may be used or reproduced in any manner whatsoever without written permission except in the case of brief quotations embodied in critical articles or reviews. For information, address St. Martin's Press, 175 Fifth Avenue, New York, N.Y. 10010.

Library of Congress Cataloging-in-Publication Data

Astle, Richard M.
    The commonsense MBA / Richard M. Astle ; foreword by Stephen R. Covey.
        p. cm.
    ISBN 0-312-13041-4
    1. Small business—Management.   2. Entrepreneurship.
3. Strategic planning.   I. Title.
HD62.7.A768   1995
658.02'2—dc20   95-2106
                                                                        CIP

First published in the United States by The Entrepreneurial Group

First St. Martin's Griffin Edition: May 1995
10   9   8   7   6   5   4   3   2   1

The Entrepreneurial Quotient Test, copyright 1985, 1987, and 1992 was created by the Northwestern Mutual Life Insurance Company, Milwaukee, Wisconsin. Reprinted by permission.

To Teri, my wife

The Commonsense MBA

The Seven Practices of Enduring Businesses for the Entrepreneur

It don't make no difference what you do as long as you're the boss.

Mike Smith

Contents

Foreword   7

Acknowledgements 11

Introduction 13

Part 1 **Entrepreneurship in the 1990s** 15

Chapter 1 **The 80/20 Principle of Business**
Encouragement for Entrepreneurs 17

Chapter 2 **You Have Two Choices**
Employee or Employer: Which Is Best for You? . . . 29

Chapter 3 **Understanding the Process of Personal Success**
The Personal Achievement Metaphor 39

Part 2 **The Seven Practices of Enduring Businesses** . 67

Chapter 4 **Practice One: Put People First**
The Practice of Treating People Well 69

Chapter 5 **Practice Two: Do What You Say**
The Practice of Being Dependable and Punctual . . . 79

Chapter 6 **Practice Three: Build Trust**
The Practice of Developing Trust with Character and
Integrity 91

Chapter 7 **Practice Four: Put Needs before Wants**
The Practice of Using Prudence and Restraint in the
Handling of Business and Personal Finances 107

Chapter 8   **Practice Five: Do It Well**
The Practice of Delivering Good Quality and Total
Customer Service 131

Chapter 9   **Practice Six: Don't Embark without a Map**
The Practice of Implementing Basic Business Planning
from the Start 151

Chapter 10   **Practice Seven: Sell, Sell, Sell**
The Practice of Having a Constant Strategy for
Marketing and Sales 163

Afterword 173

Appendix A **Business Plan for Submission to Lenders** 175

Appendix B **Informal Business Plan for Use by the Owner** . . 229

Appendix C **Business Start-up Checklist** 235

Bibliography 241

Index 245

Foreword

by Stephen R. Covey

Richard Astle and I share a deep belief in the inherent capacity of people to be self-aware, creative, resourceful, and proactive. Richard writes about "Seven Practices of Enduring Businesses," and I write about "Seven Habits of Highly Effective People." And while we both believe in the tremendous value of education, we also recognize that much of our real learning comes after our formal education. As Mark Twain said, you should "never let schooling interfere with your education." Renewing our intellectual capital is a never-ending, life-long process.

Richard, too, sees the importance of building trust on the basis of trustworthy character. However, he puts greater emphasis on the "common sense" and obvious factors that significantly improve an entrepreneur's chances for success. These factors include a ceaseless dedication to dependability, punctuality, fidelity to one's word, prudence, and financial restraint.

We both speak of a curious phenomenon—people climbing the ladder of success only to discover that it's leaning against the wrong wall.

Indeed, many people these days are climbing faster and better, and they are getting nowhere more efficiently. Still others live with the illusion that what they want is what they need, and that achieving what they want will lead to happiness and fulfillment. And it often isn't until they reach the top rung that they finally face the reality behind their illusions and see that there's something beyond their misplaced values that impacts their quality of life. Only then do they wake up to discover their shattered relationships or long-lost moments of rich living in the wake of their once intense efforts aimed at bringing recognition or financial reward.

Many of these people have deep desires to increase personal and professional effectiveness. They begin to sense that there are better ways to do things—and maybe better things to do—to bring about quality results. But one thing is for sure: if we keep doing what we're doing, we'll keep getting what we've always gotten. One definition of insanity is "to keep doing the same things and expect different results."

Encouragement and Wisdom

In this book, Richard Astle offers encouragement to entrepreneurs who often live in perpetual crisis as they respond to midnight wake-up calls and midday client and employee "fire alarms." He also offers wisdom—an invitation to listen to that inner sense that is not so common in the day-to-day practice of business.

Richard notes that certain things *are* fundamental to business success, just as certain things are basic to human fulfillment and quality of life. If these "first things" are not put first, we can expect to feel empty, incomplete, and unfulfilled. Strength in our capacity to live, to love, to learn, and to leave a legacy cannot be faked. It must be nurtured over time by our actions and decisions. By consistently putting the first things first, we become more empowered to lead our lives, not just manage our time.

Just as real as "true north" is in the physical world, so the timeless laws of cause and effect operate in the world of personal effectiveness and human interaction. The collective wisdom of the ages reveals these "true north" principles as recurring themes, foundational to every great person or society. Creating and sustaining quality of life is a function of aligning our beliefs and behaviors with these "true north" principles.

If our current "direction of travel" is not in alignment with these principles, then it will take real humility and self-awareness to subordinate our value-based maps to a principle-centered compass. Even then, Richard would say, only constant vigilance will keep us on the right path. Those who fail to regularly check their position with these compasses will soon see their clients, together with their profits, head south for a very long winter. When we recognize that external verities and realities ultimately govern, we ought to willingly align with them all our roles and goals, plans and activities.

No More Crisis Management

Reading Richard's book gives us a sure way out of crisis management. His "seven practices" are based on what I call the timeless "agricultural principles."

In agriculture, we can easily see that natural laws and principles govern the work and determine the harvest. But in social and corporate cultures, we somehow think we can dismiss natural processes, cheat the system, and still win the day. Indeed, there is much evidence to support our belief.

For example, did you ever "cram" in school—goof off during the semester—and then spend all night before the big test trying to cram a semester's worth of learning into your head?

I'm ashamed to admit it, but I crammed my way through undergraduate school, thinking I was really clever because I could psych out the system by learning what the teacher wanted. "How does she grade? If she grades mostly on lectures, then I don't have to worry about reading the text. What about this other class? We have to read the book? Okay, where are the Cliff Notes so I can get a quick summary instead?" I wanted the grade, but I didn't want it to crimp my lifestyle.

Then I got into the MBA program at Harvard Business School—a different league altogether. I spent my first three months cramming to make up for four years of academic negligence, and I wound up in the hospital with ulcerated colitis. I was trying to short-cut natural processes, and I found out that it doesn't work.

Richard's book is a swift kick out of the comfort zone for those who live by cramming and the "quick fix." He writes about the natural process of personal success. He teaches us that even though in the short term cramming and quick fixes appear to work in school or business, these won't work well in any system for the long term. If the laws of a country, city, family, or company are not in sync with natural laws and timeless principles, we can expect that people will resort to doing their own thing.

If we cram in school, we may get grades and degrees—even MBAs —but we won't get a quality education. We eventually discover a difference between economic or political success in a social system and true success in life. The latter requires what Richard calls the "MBA" of common sense—the ability to think analytically and creatively, to communicate verbally and in writing, to cross borders and solve problems. These are skills that every entrepreneur needs, in spades.

Center of Correct Principles and Practices

Richard Astle keeps us focused on the differences between wants and needs, faith and fear, positive and negative, humility and pride. Humility, in my experience, comes from knowing that principles ultimately govern—and that we're only effective to the degree we discover and live in harmony with them. With humility, we can cultivate the attitudes and habits of continual learning. We become involved in an ongoing quest to understand and live in harmony with the Laws of Life. We don't get caught up in the arrogance of values, which blinds us to self-awareness and makes us insensitive to conscience.

Our security is not based on our possessions, positions, and credentials, or on comparisons with others; instead, our security comes from our own integrity to "true north" principles.

Whenever we fail or make a mistake or hit a principle head-on, we say, "What can I learn from this experience?" As we learn where we went wrong, we can turn weaknesses into strengths.

"What I like about experience," wrote C. S. Lewis, "is that it is such an honest thing. You may have deceived yourself, but experience is not trying to deceive you. The universe rings true wherever you fairly test it."

With the humility that comes from being principle-centered, we can better learn from the past, have hope for the future, and act with confidence, not arrogance, in the present. Arrogance is lack of self-awareness, blindness, an illusion, a false form of self-confidence, and a false sense that we're somehow above the Laws of Life. Real confidence is anchored in the quiet assurance that if we act based on true principles, we will produce quality-of-life results. It's confidence born of character and competence.

Ultimately, it is not the MBA or any other degree declared by simple diplomae that will determine your success. It is the Commonsense MBA—a degree that builds upon formal education through real world experience and the patient adherence to timeless principles, and then demonstrated by trust and integrity. This leads not only to entrepreneurial success and achievement, but to true life enrichment and personal happiness.

Studying this material will reconvince you that what is common sense is not always common practice.

Acknowledgements

I was encouraged to accomplish this work by the many people I have discussed these subjects with through the years. There were clients, friends, mentors, students, family, and the general public who didn't even know that they were helping me formulate ideas I could later use to teach and encourage entrepreneurs. And there was my wife, Teri, who not only encouraged, but found the time to help with ideas and editing during her busy, full-time schedule of caring for our family: Chad, Gavin, Brandon, Garrit, Tawn, Tressa, Dane, Paityn, and Tristan.

My parents are great examples of the principles taught in this book. Some of those examples are cited herein. I will be eternally grateful for their lifelong support, encouragement, and example.

I would like to express my appreciation to those who gave their valuable input: Ron Astle, Bud Lethbridge, Bob Donaldson, Lee Fugal, Richard Allen, Lynn Stratford, and Joe Ollivier.

Thanks also to my friend and mentor, Stephen R. Covey, one of the most insightful and principled people I know. He is truly inspired and inspiring.

I am indebted to Jim Liddle for his assistance in editing the manuscript and preparing the book for publication. He has been an invaluable aid in the formulation and writing of this book.

Introduction

common sense: ordinary good sense or sound practical judgment
Webster's New World Dictionary

If you have ever contemplated going into business for yourself, this book is for you. If you have a business now that needs a little boost, if you are a victim of "right-sizing," or if you are just plain unsatisfied with your present job or situation, this book is for you. It is meant to encourage entrepreneurship. There are plenty of opportunities for striking out on your own, and it is not as difficult as you may have been led to believe. All you need is common sense.

You may think that the road is difficult, requiring specialized education, experience, and lots of money. The fact is, many successful entrepreneurs have little or no education, little or no experience in what they started, and often, little or no money for start-up. They just had the desire, did it, and then looked back and wished they had done it earlier.

Is this a good time to start a business of your own? Part 1 is my answer to that question based on my twenty years in business, my university business studies, and my association with clients and business contacts.

I started my little service business just over twenty years ago with very little money and no experience, but lots of desire and just plain common sense. The first month we did fifty-three dollars in gross revenues, and eventually we were doing over a million dollars a year. In chapter 1 I will explain about my business experience and how I discovered another application for the 80/20 principle. It applies to business and asserts that almost anyone can compete in today's market world with a business of their own.

Chapter 2 discusses everyone's two basic choices—you can work for others or you can work for yourself. Learn about the freedom of the latter alternative. Since self-employment may not be for everyone, you can test your EQ (Entrepreneurial Quotient) to see if you fit the mold.

Each of us must organize our personal lives before we can begin the process of working for ourselves and forming our own company. In chapter 3, you will learn that success is different for each individual. It is a process with a well-defined set of steps that must be followed in order to reach any goal—losing weight, changing a personality trait, putting on your pants, or even starting your own business.

Part 2 is the essence of the 80/20 Principle of Business. It is the reason that starting and having your own business may be easier than you think. If I were asked what it really takes to be successful in a business in the 1990s, this would be my answer. I devote a separate chapter to each of the Seven Practices of Enduring Businesses, which I formulated after years of research and experience. They are the essence of the Commonsense MBA.

This book is meant to encourage entrepreneurship. You don't need much money, you don't need to be fully staffed, you don't need fancy offices and cars, and you don't need an MBA. You don't even need experience. You just have to want to do it. Most people already have the experience they need by virtue of their life experiences, interpersonal relationships, and common sense.

This information is not meant as a temporary psych-up, quick-fix manual, teaching that all you need is a positive mental attitude. Nor is it a get-rich-quick book with the secret to instant wealth. This book teaches that you reap only what you sow. But it teaches that anyone who wants to sow the seeds of success and opportunity can reap the benefits, no matter what their background or education.

It is true that if people are taught correct principles and values, they can govern themselves in the day-to-day tasks of running a business. The information in this book represents more of a lesson in the commonsense principles, attitudes and practices essential to running a small business. However, an effort has also been made to direct the start-up entrepreneur by providing some detailed assistance with business plans and a checklist for starting a small business.

What is found here is the same information I like to give people I consult with when they are thinking about starting a new business. It is encouragement. What a great feeling it is to be running your own business! If this book turns out to be the encouragement you need to go forward with your entrepreneurial plans, it will all be worth it. Don't hesitate to let me know. I think you will be surprised when you read how easy it is. This book should encourage you to recognize that all you need is a Commonsense MBA.

Part 1

Entrepreneurship in the 1990s

If you were to ask my opinion about going into a business of your own in the 1990s, this would be my answer to you.

Chapter 1

The 80/20 Principle of Business

Encouragement for Entrepreneurs

principle: a natural or original tendency; a fundamental truth, law, doctrine or motivating force, upon which others are based.

Webster's New World Dictionary

The American Dream

Go back with me to about September 1972. I had graduated from college with a bachelor's degree in accounting, and I planned to attend law school part-time while I started my family. I had gotten married that summer, so I needed a good job. I hired into a large insurance company in the Los Angeles area as a personal injury adjuster. I investigated accident cases and negotiated injury accident claims with attorneys.

I felt lucky. My time was basically my own. I was given cases to handle and settle. I had a company car, an expense account, and I simply had to keep my work up so I would look good during the periodic case review. I felt good about life, driving around in my new company car with my suit and tie. I remember driving up alongside families with old cars thinking I was really lucky. I was glad I had gotten my degree, which was required for this "good" job. I felt successful.

All of that "greatness" wore off within two years. I quickly figured out I would not be able to support my family in this job, not even for the length of time it would take me to finish law school. Even if I decided to make the company a career and moved through the ranks of supervisor, manager, regional manager, etc., I wouldn't be happy. None of those guys made what I wanted to make, and they weren't doing what I wanted to do. They still had bosses to report to and orders to follow. They still had to be at work at a certain time. They had to go where they were needed within the company area even if they had to move their families to another city. And, of course, what if I were to spend ten or fifteen years building a career, only to find the company "right-sizing" me right out of a job?

When the manager was in a bad mood, he took it out on us, the adjusters. We had to report to work on certain days by a certain time, for no apparent reason. When the work load was heavy, we had to spend extra time keeping it current. I feel for those with a nine-to-five job, and I have never understood the policy of some companies who pay their people salaries but require that they work extra hours for no extra pay.

I knew I wanted independence and freedom. After doing a stint in the U.S. Army and Vietnam, I knew for sure that I didn't want bosses telling me what to do every day, and I was sure I couldn't live with having someone else choose where my family had to move the next year. I also knew I wanted to make more money, and working for somebody else was not the way to do that.

Most of all, I wanted to reap the rewards of working hard to build a business. I had learned somewhere that when you work for somebody else, you build equity in the business for somebody else, the owner. When you have your own business, your efforts, and the efforts of your employees, build equity for you.

Even though I was young and inexperienced (I was still in my twenties), I began to feel the lure of self-employment. I had been thinking about making a move but didn't know what to do. I had been watching other service companies I had dealt with as an adjuster, trying to figure out what made some of them successful and the others fail. I was thinking in terms of filling a community need, but I didn't want to face a lot of competition.

I remember the day very clearly. It was in September 1972. I was sitting at my desk feeling sorry for myself and daydreaming. I clearly was unsatisfied with what I was doing. Something told me to make an announcement to the others in the room. There were a few other adjusters in the open room at their desks working. I turned my chair slightly to the side, put my feet up on my desk, leaned back in my chair, folded my arms, turned my head toward those in the room and announced I was going into a business of my own, and that I would be gone within one year.

Someone asked, "What are you going to do?" I said I didn't know. They laughed. We all turned back to our desks and I said nothing more on the subject until I gave notice five months later. Thirty days after that I was gone.

I had started a service business a month after I made the announcement. I did it part-time while keeping up my adjuster job. When the business got to the point where I was too busy, and where I could consider myself to be making a living at it, I gave notice and left.

When I gave notice, the other adjusters to whom I made the original announcement were surprised to hear that I was in the legal investigation and photocopy service business for insurance companies and attorneys. This was one of the services we adjusters hired from outside firms. It was a simple service, one about which I knew nothing. I figured out what needed to be done in a very short time. It took very little capital to start. I figured all I needed to do was perform a good service for a fair price, and I would get my share of the market.

Their comments were just what you would expect. "Aren't there already plenty of people doing that? Seems like there is too much competition out there." There was some discussion in the office about how I would do. Much of it was negative. I do remember one important comment. It was that I would probably do well since all of the legal photocopying services we now employed as adjusters in that area were flakes.

I said, "Bingo!"

He had hit the nail right on the head. That is exactly what my intention was. I didn't care how many people were already doing it. And there were a lot of people in the business. I had to ignore the competition completely. Most of the outside firms doing what I was doing were late with delivery, often messed up the assignments we gave them, had bad attitudes when you tried to communicate with them, and couldn't be trusted.

It was then that I first began to think 80/20. At least 80% of my competitors were giving poor service. Sure, there were a lot of people doing what I was doing, but I really only had to compete with 20% of them. All I had to do was provide what they didn't: quality work, timely delivery, a good attitude, and an honest, fair billing. I figured if I did that, I would get my market share no matter how much competition there was. After all, weren't 80% of the potential clients looking for another service to use? I planned to be their man.

It was a thrill to start it. I had business cards, order forms and envelopes printed with my company name on them. I made up custom invoices tailored to my needs. I got a checkbook and opened a set of books using a single entry, cash basis system for simplicity. At first it was fun to keep the books myself. I filed a fictitious name statement at the county, got the necessary licenses, and I was in business. I was excited to go around the city and perform the details I would have hated doing for someone else. It truly was an exciting experience. When asked, "Where are you employed, sir?" or "What do you do for a living?" I could say with pride, "I own a legal service business."

My first month I grossed $53. The next month I did $73. By the end of the first half year I was making a living. I added services and clients. The business continued to grow each year until it was doing over a million dollars a year. I had to work hard, handle the usual business problems and suffer through some rough days, but I also got to enjoy many good days. I did a lot of things when the business was growing that I didn't think college-educated guys should have to do. Later, when I hired others to do that work, I enjoyed the business much more. But I owned it, I was building up my own equity for a later sale, I made good money, I seldom dreaded getting up to go to work, and no one ever bossed me around. My office was always either in my home or within one mile of it. I ran that business for eighteen years until I sold it.

After very little time in business I knew I had figured out how easy a small business is to start and operate. Can I be so bold as to say it was almost like operating without competition? That's about the way it is when you only have to worry about 20% of your competition. I was learning a lot while building my business, lessons I had not heard anything about previously, not even in college.

I began to put my facts together and soon became convinced that there was a lesson to be learned out there in the business world that most business owners, professors, and motivational writers weren't talking much about. Call it what you want, but there is a principle (rule, doctrine, formula...) that makes starting your own business relatively simple.

The 80/20 Principle of Business

I like to call it the 80/20 Principle of Business. It is for current as well as potential business owners. It means simply that a large percentage of people (80%) never take the simple steps necessary to achieve their desires. That is why most people work for others and are not prepared for retirement. The principle also means that most (80%) businesses don't practice certain simple, commonsense principles that the enduring, successful businesses follow. The principle means that there is little competition in either the personal or the business lives of people. It doesn't mean that personal achievement or business success is easy. It just means that it is not as competitive as you may think. It doesn't require genius or an MBA. And it is well within the reach of anyone who has a bit of common sense. There is plenty of room for success, no matter how many are making it personally or professionally.

Everyone thinks occasionally about what would be the ideal business to go into at a particular time in history. If you time it properly, there are always businesses that can make you rich. But those opportunities often go away quickly, so those who hit it just right can do well only for a while.

The Foolproof Formula

What particular business is good right now? Where do the best opportunities lie for the 1990s? The answer is that there are certain businesses that are good any time. They are based on high demand and good service rather than the fact that there may be a temporarily good economy at the moment. For those who are pursuing a plan to become self-employed but don't know exactly what kind of business to start, consider the following formula which can apply almost anytime to almost anyone. Here is the formula:

Choose a simple, high-demand service business. These kinds of services require little training or capital to start and are services used by most people and businesses everywhere. Don't be concerned about competition, since many or most of those doing it are not performing well. Use the Seven Practices of Enduring Businesses by treating people well, being dependable and punctual, building trust by being honest, managing your money with prudence and operating without debt, giving quality, using a flexible business plan, and constantly marketing your service to prospective customers. Use common sense and start slowly, growing naturally as business expands. Be cautious. Perform all business functions yourself, part-time at first while you keep your other job, if you can. Be a sole-proprietorship, and keep your books on the cash basis for simplicity. This formula is the essence of the 80/20 Principle of Business.

Foolproof Formula Examples

Here is a list of examples that fit the mold of the above formula. Remember, these are businesses that have a high demand, cost little to start, require no extensive education or genius, can be done part-time to get started, don't require expensive facilities, and require only the practice of the principles discussed in this book to compete and get your market share. These businesses can make you more money than many attorneys you know. This partial list is made only for purposes of showing examples and giving ideas. It is not exhaustive. By reading over the list you will get an idea of those kinds of businesses that almost anyone can start and find success. Make up your own list with those areas of the business world with which you are most familiar.

Accounting and bookkeeping
Addressing and letter services
Apartment maintenance
Appliance repair
Attorney support services, including legal research
Auto repair and all related services
Auto detailing and cleaning
Banquet consulting
Bicycle repair
Blacktop painting
Boat repair
Bodyguard service
Building contractors—all contracting, sub-contracting, and related
    services

Building inspection
Building maintenance
Business consulting
Child care
Chimney cleaning and repair
Cleaning services—residential and commercial
Clerical office service
Computer related services—including graphics, publishing, consulting, training, service and repair, etc.
Consulting—all areas
Courier service
Credit and debt counseling
Debt collection
Decorating, interior, and other related services
Delivery service
Domestic help
Drafting service
Fumigating
Genealogy service
Gift buying service
Glass repair
Graphic design
Handyman service
Home inspection service
House cleaning
Income tax service
Janitor service
Lawn and grounds maintenance
Lawn mower repair
Management consulting
Motorcycle repair and service
Office machine repair
Office support service
Polishing service
Presentation
Private investigation
Process serving
Property maintenance

Ranges and ovens—service and repair
Real estate—all related services including brokers, agents, inspections,
    loans, etc.
Recreational vehicle repair and service
Refinishing
Remodeling service
Research services—all fields
Snow removal service
Stereo repair and service
Swimming pool service and repair
Television and radio service and repair
Tree service
Typing service
Upholstery cleaning
Vacuum cleaners—service and repair
Washing machines and dryers—service and repair
Window cleaning

Small Business Statistics

In my counseling of prospective entrepreneurs, I am often asked about the failure rate of new businesses. I always tell them that the answer should have nothing to do with them or their decision to start a business. Nevertheless, a discussion of such questions is interesting and enlightening, but it should not be discouraging.

How many small businesses do fail? How often do they fail? When do they fail? What exactly is a small business? These are some of the questions most frequently asked about small businesses. I wish I had accurate answers, but unfortunately there are none. The problem is that there is no comprehensive system of accounting to provide the answers. Government statistics are estimates from sources like the IRS's tax return data.

Research from a variety of sources, including government documents and the reports of the Small Business Administration to Congress, shows the following:

1. The number of new start-up businesses per year in the United States has recently risen to over a million.

2. There may be as many as forty million self-employed people in the United States today.

3. About 75% of all small businesses have no employees except the owner and perhaps the owner's spouse.

4. Statistics are generally tracked by the number of employees a business has. Since the majority of small businesses have no employees, such tracking is difficult.

5. Small businesses are creating the most jobs.

6. There is no standard definition of a small business. The size of a business may be measured in terms of a number of things, like employees, assets, or revenues. For most statistical purposes, the Small Business Administration's Office of Advocacy defines small businesses in terms of the average size of a business in that industry.

7. According to the IRS, 21% of all business tax returns are filed by corporations, 9% by partnerships and 69% by sole proprietorships.

8. No complete list of new start-ups or business failures is available.

9. Anywhere from 72% to 97% of new businesses fail at some time after start-up. The most reliable figures show that 80% fail in the first five years, 50% of the remaining businesses fail in the next five years, and there are only around 5% that endure past the twelve-year mark. Don't forget, however, that many of these businesses that "fail" are actually successful businesses that the owner chooses to retire from without selling. (And remember also, that contained in this book .are the commonsense practices that make such failures easily avoidable.)

10. Variations in self-employment figures can be explained by the interplay of four factors:

a. Demand

Self-employment is more common in such industries as service, retail trade and construction than in mining and manufacturing. This is partly because of the large amount of capital required to start a business in heavy industry. Also, people are more likely to start businesses in industries in which they have work experience. Business opportunities are opening up because of the increased demand for the products that self-employed people can offer.

b. Experience in the labor force

The longer people have been in the work force, the longer they have had to accumulate assets and experience that can be valuable in the transition to self-employment. Also, they are more familiar with the business opportunities available in their field of expertise.

c. Formal education

Because self-employment is more common in many of the traditional professions such as medicine and law, people with graduate educations are more likely to be self-employed. These statistics can be misleading, because many very successful entrepreneurs have little formal education at all.

d. Economic climate

Cyclical changes in the economy and changes in taxes and interest rates all affect the rate of self-employment. Taxes are an important consideration in choosing between self-employment and wage work. It is easier for self-employed people to take advantage of the tax laws. Interest rates affect the way prospective business owners get financing. Cyclical changes in the economy affect the number of self-employment opportunities.

It is clear that the time is right for entrepreneurial thinking. Even President Clinton has said that this will be the decade of the entrepreneur. Leaders in the field of entrepreneurial literature say that sales of their products and services are going up. Many people who have been laid off from what they considered secure jobs are now considering businesses of their own, and the economy is poised for an upswing. There truly isn't a better time.

In Summary

Don't hesitate any longer looking for that easy, get-rich-quick opportunity that has to be timed just right. There is a whole world full of opportunities right now if you understand the 80/20 Principle of Business.

For reasons yet to be understood, which are the subject of continued research, people who start businesses don't perform well. They don't treat people well or fairly, they aren't punctual and dependable, and they endanger their financial future by spending unwisely. Take advantage of the opportunities available to anyone with common sense. Go ahead and compete. Customers will come out of the woodwork. You won't believe how they'll line up to pay you for your services and products. You will wish you had done it sooner.

Start your engines. You are in for the ride of your life!

Chapter 2

You Have Two Choices

Employee or Employer: Which Is Best for You?

We hold these truths to be self-evident, that all men are created equal; that they are endowed by their Creator with certain unalienable rights; that among these are life, liberty and the pursuit of happiness.

Thomas Jefferson, *The Declaration of Independence*

Making Money

There are two ways to acquire money. It can be given to you by gift or inheritance, or you can get it the old fashioned way, by earning it. For most of us, dreaming about the gift or inheritance from a long lost relative method may be enjoyable, but it is a waste of time. Let's face it: we will have to earn the money.

There are two ways to earn money. You make money with your money, and you can make money with your efforts. Proper investments can earn great rewards, but it takes money to do it. People who have spare funds to play with certainly should, and usually do, have that money well invested. For the purposes of the subject at hand, we will concentrate on the latter method of earning money—with our efforts.

There are two ways to earn money with your efforts. You can work for someone else, or you can work for yourself. And I suppose we shouldn't leave out the option to do both.

The American Dream

Many people are advocates of the option to work for yourself, to be an entrepreneur. They have some fairly strong feelings about how our system directs people to work for others. Most of us dream the American dream of owning our own homes, making good money, being financially independent and secure, and even owning our own business and being our own boss. That, to many of us, is freedom—the freedom to choose for ourselves.

From our earliest childhood we learn about what a blessing it is to be American, to be free to do what we want to do in life. We have a choice in this country. No one tells us what we will do or where we will work. We literally can choose for ourselves. As far back as I can remember, a quotation from the Declaration of Independence has meant a lot to me. It says, "We hold these truths to be self-evident, that all men are created equal; that they are endowed by their Creator with certain unalienable right; that among these are life, liberty and the pursuit of happiness."

Each individual is free to pursue this happiness in his own way. And to each, happiness may have a different definition. We all have our own personal circumstances, desires, and goals. Happiness seems to coincide closely with the definition of success. Happiness is what each individual wants for himself, differing according to desires or inclinations. And we are free to pursue it without interference from any source—government or individual. As I have mentioned before, not everyone is suited to be in business for himself. Some people should remain employees and be the best part of their company team they can be. But we all have the choice, and we should all be aware of the great opportunity that this great country affords us.

Self-determination—what a concept! Just think of it. In parts of the world, this concept is not even imagined by its people. No choice, no imagination, no thinking for themselves. No ability to act, just to be acted upon. Think of it: we can think for ourselves. We have the power to start the motor and shift the gears along the process of success and pursue happiness and the good life. What a great blessing.

Programmed to Work for Others

It is sad to think that some people don't take advantage of this great opportunity. From the time we are children we are taught about this privilege of freedom of choice, but at the same time we are programmed by well-meaning people to work hard for others. Parents teach their children the work ethic: to work hard, and that by working hard, success and happiness will follow. Schools and universities teach students to prepare for that all-important interview. Business management schools, and yes, even entrepreneur schools, fail to teach people about the great success and happiness that can result from working for yourself. They readily admit that it is not in their goals and mission statements. "It is not our job," they say.

Tell me that the pursuit of happiness and the good life consists of going to work each day to a job that is either boring or lacks challenge, where the people are not treated with dignity, where people work hard to build someone else's business equity and then are given a gold watch and a swift kick in the pants at a good-bye company party when they leave. Tell me that it is pursuing happiness to know that you have a limit, a ceiling, to what you can make, and that you never know when you may be given the proverbial pink slip and be out on the street looking for another job just like the last one.

"Our People Are Our Greatest Asset"

We have all heard our bosses say that their greatest asset is their people, their employees. The next time they say that to you, ask them to show you on the balance sheet where that great asset is located. Current and fixed assets consist of cash or its equivalent and the other items in a business that represent things owned by the company. Subtract the liabilities owed against the assets, and you have the company's net worth.

Then where are the people, the greatest asset the owner says he has and owes so much to, located on the financial statements of the company? The answer is that they are located on the income statement under "expenses." It is called "salaries" expense. Ask any accountant. It's an expense item. Expenses are those items the owner tries to keep down, to minimize. The income statement lists the revenues the company acquired over a certain period and then deducts the expenses of the same period to determine the net income the company made for the period. The idea in business is to keep the revenues up by pushing for more sales and to lower the expenses by cutting costs. One way to cut expenses is to negotiate the lowest possible salaries and wages. Owners will tell you that the employee is their greatest asset, but you had better believe that it is their desire, even their fiduciary duty, to pay the lowest wages that the market will bear.

It is not difficult to slant the pursuit of happiness toward working for yourself. Too many great people who are capable, talented, and educated have the ability to be their own boss, but instead they go directly to a job that they are doomed from the outset to dislike. Often they end up unhappy.

Entrepreneurship in College

Many colleges and universities are beginning to develop entrepreneurship programs. The Small Business Administration indicates that entrepreneurship education has experienced unprecedented growth over the past fifteen years. In a survey conducted in 1985 (National Survey of Entrepreneurial Education) the SBA says that the number of schools teaching entrepreneurship has grown from none just twenty years ago to over four hundred in 1985. This includes high schools and four-year colleges. Even though it has come a long way in the past twenty or thirty years, the field has not reached its proper position of maturity. Many schools only have one or two courses available, and studies show that their courses are relatively thin in quality and depth. A preliminary investigation shows that the subjects discussed in these programs don't differ that much from the usual business management program that prepares students to enter the field of management as employees. But let's give them credit. Entrepreneurial subjects are appearing, and slants toward entrepreneurship are becoming part of undergraduate and postgraduate programs in many universities. They appear to be concluding that this may be the decade of the entrepreneur.

The slow progress of entrepreneurial programs may be due in part to the lack of theories, models, research studies, or methods. The practices described in this book would make good methods and models. But tell college professors to teach honesty and trust as a means to increased profits and see what they say. Putting people before bottom-line profits can't be found in many textbooks.

Entrepreneurs are leaders. They are opportunity takers. They are not followers. They set policy for others to follow. Many college professors have not worked as business managers, and many have not started and operated their own businesses. Before there can be a great deal of progress in entrepreneurial programs at colleges and universities, someone will have to establish a cadre of academic faculty members that are committed to entrepreneurship.

Studying business management today leaves many students disenchanted with the traditional big-business-oriented programs. It's no wonder that most business management students have no loftier goal than to get a good job. What else can they do? They have been taught only to take a small management position in a large corporation after studying concepts that only apply to large organizations.

The Pressure Is On

Pressures from students, the government, and the media in the 1980s has created demand for emphasis on entrepreneurship education. There is also pressure due to the current trend of "right-sizing" by many larger companies. Many companies are looking at operating with fewer employees, consolidating functions, and downsizing staff. Many will not be hiring as many people even when the 1990s recession ends. This pressure will begin to show up in programs at universities around the world. The Small Business Administration concludes from its many surveys, beginning in 1979 and extending throughout the 1980s, that entrepreneurship education is on the rise and is not likely to subside in the near future. The demand is too high. Colleges and universities will have to respond. This is clearly the era of entrepreneurship, not only in the United States, but in Eastern Europe and other countries where new opportunities now abound.

It Is Never Too Late

Some people may think it is too late for them to go into business for themselves. This is a sad commentary. Many people have always had the self-employment bug. Employment has almost never been an option for them. Sometimes it is a result of their upbringing, watching their parents operate their own business. But people should never consider it to be too late. My father started law school when he was thirty-six, passed the bar at forty, and practiced law by himself for about thirty-five years. I have heard of people starting law school in their fifties and beyond. Businesses are started by people of all ages. And most of them will tell you they wish they had done it earlier.

Should You Be an Entrepreneur?

Studies of successful entrepreneurs reveal common characteristics—family backgrounds, experiences, motivations, personality traits, behaviors, values, and beliefs. How do you fit these patterns? What is your EQ (Entrepreneurial Quotient)?

Northwestern Mutual Life has created a small leaflet distributed by their representatives which contains a test to predict how suited you are to entrepreneurship. This test can't predict your success—it can only give you an idea whether you will have a head start or a handicap with which to work. Entrepreneurial skills can be learned. The test is intended to help you see how you compare with others who have been successful entrepreneurs.

Here goes. Add or subtract from your score as you evaluate yourself.

1. Significantly high numbers of entrepreneurs are children of first-generation Americans. If your parents immigrated to the United States, score one. If not, score minus one.
2. Successful entrepreneurs are not, as a rule, top achievers in school. If you were a top student, subtract four. If not, add four.
3. Entrepreneurs are not especially enthusiastic about participating in group activities in school. If you enjoyed group activities—clubs, team sports, double dates—subtract one. If not, add one.
4. Studies of entrepreneurs show that, as youngsters, they often preferred to be alone. Did you prefer to be alone as a youngster? If so, add one. If not, subtract one.
5. Those who started enterprises during childhood—lemonade stands, family newspapers, greeting card sales—or ran for elected office at school can add two, because enterprise usually

can be traced to an early age. If you didn't initiate enterprises, subtract two.

6. Stubbornness as a child seems to translate into determination to do things one's own way—a hallmark of proven entrepreneurs. If you were a stubborn child, add one. If not, subtract one.

7. Caution may involve an unwillingness to take risks, a handicap for those embarking on previously uncharted territory. Were you cautious as a youngster? If yes, deduct four. If no, add four.

8. If you were daring or adventuresome, add four more.

9. Entrepreneurs often have the faith to pursue different paths despite the opinions of others. If the opinions of others matter a lot to you, subtract one. If not, add one.

10. Being tired of a daily routine often precipitates an entrepreneur's decision to start an enterprise. If changing your daily routine would be an important motivation for starting your own enterprise, add two. If not, subtract two.

11. Yes, you really enjoy work. But are you willing to work overnight? If yes, add two. If no, subtract six.

12. If you are willing to work as long as it takes with little or no sleep to finish a job, add four more.

13. Entrepreneurs generally enjoy their type of work so much they move from one project to another—nonstop. When you complete a project successfully, do you immediately start another? If yes, add two. If no, subtract two.

14. Successful entrepreneurs are willing to use their savings to finance a project. If you are willing to commit your savings to start a business, add two. If not, subtract two.

15. Would you also be willing to borrow from others? Then add two more. If not, subtract two.

16. If your business should fail, would you immediately work on starting another? If yes, add four. If no, subtract four.

17. Or, if you would immediately start looking for a job with a regular paycheck, subtract one more.

18. Do you believe being an entrepreneur is risky? If yes, subtract two. If no, add two.

19. Many entrepreneurs put their long-term and short-term goals in writing. If you do, add one. If you don't, subtract one.

20. Handling cash flow can be critical to entrepreneurial success. Do you believe you have the ability to deal with cash flow in a professional manner? If so, add two. If not, subtract two.
21. Entrepreneurial personalities seem to be easily bored. If you are easily bored, add two. If not, subtract two.
22. Optimism can fuel the drive to press for success in uncharted waters. If you're an optimist, add two. Pessimist, subtract two.

What's your EQ?

If you scored +35 or more, you have everything going for you. You ought to achieve spectacular entrepreneurial success (barring acts of God or other variables beyond your control).

If you scored +15 to +34, your background, skills and talents give you excellent chances for success in your own business. You should go far.

If you scored 0 to +15, you have a head start of ability and/or experience in running a business and ought to be successful in opening an enterprise of your own if you apply yourself and learn the necessary skills to make it happen.

If you scored 0 to -15, you might be able to make a go of it if you ventured on your own, but you would have to work extra hard to compensate for a lack of built-in advantages and skills that give others a leg up in beginning their own businesses.

If you scored -15 to -43, your talents probably lie elsewhere. You ought to consider whether building your own business is what you really want to do, because you may find yourself swimming against the tide if you make the attempt. Another work arrangement—working for a company or for someone else, or developing a career in a profession or an area of technical expertise—may be far more congenial to you and allow you to enjoy a lifestyle appropriate to your abilities and interests.

Other Characteristics

You also may want to consider what the Small Business Administration calls a self-analysis to determine whether you have the characteristics of a successful entrepreneur. Members of SCORE (Service Corps Of Retired Executives) have put together a checklist of such characteristics:

1. Are you a leader?
2. Do you like to make your own decisions?
3. Do others turn to you for help in making decisions?
4. Do you enjoy competition?
5. Do you have willpower and self-discipline?
6. Do you plan ahead?
7. Do you like people?
8. Do you get along well with others?

Identifying Your Reasons

One step that is often overlooked is to ask yourself why you want to own your own business. Do the following reasons apply to you?

1. Being free from the nine-to-five daily work routine.
2. Being your own boss.
3. Doing what you want when you want to do it.
4. Improving your standard of living.
5. Escaping the boredom of your current job.
6. Selling a product or service for which you feel there is a demand.

In Summary

It is never too late to start thinking for yourself instead of merely reacting. Even though you have been programmed throughout your life by parents, friends, and most of the people around you to get a job and become one of the company's greatest assets, you can pull out that diskette, erase it, and write yourself a new program. You be the programmer; you make the choice. Think for yourself. Keep your job and be a part of that company and be happy there. Or start your own business and seek the freedom and happiness that is your great privilege as an American. It's your choice: employee or employer. No matter what your past experience and training, consider the fact that you have two options. You always have, and you always will.

Chapter 3

Understanding the Process of Personal Success

The Personal Achievement Metaphor

process: a particular method of doing something, generally involving a number of steps or operations; a continuing development involving many changes.
Webster's New World Dictionary

Success

Before you can achieve success in a business of your own, you must have reached a certain level of personal organization and commitment. Business success doesn't just happen. Success is a process, not an event. This chapter deals with the process of deciding to leave your job and go into a business of your own, if that is what you want. Remember, this book is meant to encourage. Before you make the decision to go after that goal, you must understand and follow the process of personal commitment toward achievement.

A Popular Subject

Much has been said and written about personal success. How to achieve success is one of the most sellable subjects. Everyone wants it. Everyone dreams of it. But only a few people achieve their dreams of success.

Unfortunately, most of the literature on the subject either complicates or oversimplifies the process. The reader is given too many steps to follow, and those steps are often out of order. Even worse, some books claim that a simple change of attitude is all that you need to achieve overnight success. Sometimes there is too much psychological detail. People read the material and get confused or lost. They try to follow the instructions for a short time, but then they slip back into their old ways and routines. They forget what they were working on and where they were going.

The Gearshift Metaphor

I have reviewed most of the popular success literature through the years as I have set out to accomplish my own goals, including writing this book. That review, along with my own experience in achieving goals, has motivated me to create a basic five-step program of personal success. These steps encapsulate what has been said in literally hundreds of books on personal success. The metaphor of the gearshift may be new to you, but the process itself is not. As you will see, everyone is already familiar with the process. In fact, we all use it every day. I use the gearshift to illustrate the fact that personal success is a process that must be followed from step one, or first gear.

If you have driven a car before, you already know how gears work. You don't need to be an automotive engineer or a mechanic to understand it. The fact is that personal achievement is attained using the same type of process as getting an automobile from dead stop to full speed.

You can get cars with a standard transmission that you shift yourself, or you can buy them with an automatic transmission that shifts by itself as you gain speed. In any event, the transmission in a car is a compact unit usually mounted just to the rear of the engine. It contains different sizes of gears so the power of the engine can be transferred to the drive wheels (back or front) with changes of speed or force. If you leave it in first and try to get to fifty-five miles per hour on the freeway, you will take your engine above its maximum work load and burn it up fast. It doesn't work.

If you shift to second after a few seconds, the transmission changes into a higher gear and allows the car to go faster with less engine work. In the end you can be going in fifth gear at fifty-five miles per hour with the engine working no harder than when you were going twenty miles per hour in first gear.

Understand That It Is a Process

Don't worry if you don't understand it all at this point, as long as you understand the following: you must start in first gear and shift through the sequence of gears to get from dead stop to full speed ahead. You can't start in fifth, fourth, third, or second. Your car is engineered to start only in first. You must start in first, go to second, then third, then fourth, and cruise successfully along the highway in fifth. If you want to go backwards, you must stop, put it in reverse gear, and back up.

This process can be very closely compared to the process we follow to achieve any of our goals successfully. Each gear can be compared to a step in the process of personal achievement. However, before we define what each of the gears means in this context, let us briefly discuss what success is and what it means to different people.

Success Defined

Most of us at some time in our lives have wondered why some people are successful at what they do, whether as an employee or as a self-employed business owner. Those who are now successful wonder no longer. Those who are still wondering go from book to book, from psych-up self-help seminar to get-rich-quick seminar, listening to apparently successful authors and teachers complicate the process, promising results with little effort and riches just for the taking.

Success means different things to different people. Many people use the term to describe the state of a rich or prosperous individual, or one who has fame and public recognition. For instance, have you ever known someone who drove a fancy, expensive car and who lived in a very big, very nice home? You probably thought he or she must be very successful.

On the other hand, have you ever known someone who was truly rich, with lots of property paid off and businesses thriving, who drove an older car and lived in a modest house? Success may be living comfortably and having a secure future. We each define success by what we want to achieve and how we want to exist and live our lives. I have learned that you certainly can't tell what a person's net worth or yearly income is by what you see—cars, house, clothes, or jewelry. People who appear to be wealthy may actually have zero net worth (assets minus liabilities). They may be leasing the car. They may be behind in the monthly payments and might be close to having the car repossessed. The house may be close to foreclosure. And the diamonds may be fake.

Some people care about possessions and appearances; others don't. It's a matter of personal preference. To some people, being very wealthy is not worth the price of work and stress. They enjoy a life of less responsibility and less stress—and less money and fewer possessions.

For this reason, let's define success as the achievement of one's own goals or desires. Success is and must be a personal matter, to be determined by each of us in our own way. It is not a matter of comparison.

Define success in any way you wish, but consider the process to be the same no matter what your definition is. The guy who reaches his goal of having a net worth of a hundred thousand dollars is as successful as the guy whose goal was to have a million dollars. You are successful if you reach the goal you have chosen.

For that reason, it is disappointing to see people who appear to be ambitious and loaded with talent and intelligence, but who go nowhere toward achieving their goals. The sections that follow address this subject. It is the result of drawing the essential elements of the success process out of years of reading and personal experience. Some people seem intelligent and talented but lack the wisdom or common sense to follow a simple process toward their goals. The process works for any goals—family, social, personal, monetary, career—but it is especially important for those who venture into the world of entrepreneurship.

With your engine running now, you are ready to put it in first gear.

First Gear: Desire

First gear is *desire*. The first step toward any accomplishment, from the simplest of daily chores to the larger, lifelong goals, is desire. You don't put on your pants in the morning unless you want to. You don't become the president of a large corporation without first desiring it. You will not do anything until you want to. In the morning, before you get out of bed, you must want to.

Everything Begins with Desire

Understand that this rule does not mean you will always enjoy the activity, even if it is motivated by your desire. Do you always enjoy getting up in the morning or doing the dishes? It simply means that before anything is accomplished, you must want to accomplish it.

Most people will never work toward being the president of the United States, because they don't want to become president. They probably won't become the president either. Can you imagine being successful at anything, working hard at it all your life, when you hate it or don't want to make it a lifelong career? If people don't enjoy what they are doing, if they don't really want it to be their career, they seldom reach the top of that profession. They may stay with it because they want to make a living. But nothing is accomplished without first wanting it to happen.

Name Something You Want

I have asked many people, while presenting this material through the years, to name something they would like to have or do in their lifetime: something, perhaps, that they never really dreamed they would have or do. Each response was different, and nobody ever said they wanted to be president of the United States. Each person named something that was achievable. They were mostly common desires that other people had accomplished. If someone else had done it, it must be possible. It's possible even if someone else hasn't ever done it, if the person wants it badly enough.

It is clear that *the desire to achieve something carries with it the necessary ability to accomplish it.* This means that if you desire something it can be accomplished. Think of the magnitude of that statement. Call it a basic law of the world, a law of nature, a universal law, or one of God's laws. Somehow, someway, each of us can accomplish those goals and obtain those things we want. The full understanding of this natural law may not be available to all of us. But there is agreement on the theory. Everyone who responded to my question in those presentations about the one thing they desired in life can achieve the thing they want. It is within us to achieve it as surely as the desire to do it is present.

Look around You for Examples

If a person really wants to be president of the United States, it is within his or her ability. Most people don't pursue the presidency because they never get into first gear (desire). They don't want it. Look at the people who have achieved much in their lives. You probably know someone like that: the president of a large corporation, a famous person, or just a pure and simple millionaire. They may not admit it to you because they want to appear humble. They got there because they *wanted* it. Why else would they work so hard for it?

When you have a strong desire that seems to linger through the years, what you desire usually happens. Of course, there are other steps, other gears to go through to get going full speed ahead. Just understand that the first step or gear is most important. Without it at the beginning of the process, you never get on the road to success.

You May Already Be in First Gear

You probably already have a desire for something, so you have already gotten yourself into first gear. Maybe all you need to do now is to let the clutch out and give it some gas. This is evidenced, in part, by the fact that you are reading this book. It's an indication that you desire something and are searching out the path to its achievement. If you really want that sum of cash, that net worth, that personality trait, or that business of your own, learn the next step and follow up until you get what you want out of life.

Why Some Never Shift into Second

Why is it that many people have desires and dreams but never follow up and try to achieve them? Why do some people get into first gear and never shift? They get psyched up about it one day, they want to do it, they think they will someday, and they get support for the idea from other people. Then the next day they're off to work, busy with their responsibilities, and they don't do anything about it, slowly losing their enthusiasm, their interest, and often their desire.

Don't Wait One Day

You must act now to get into second gear and beyond as soon as you can. Don't wait. You are ready to proceed if you have a desire. Start today, because the longer you wait, you only get farther away from the desire, motivation, and enthusiasm.

The more difficult, more arduous, or more long-range your goal is, the more desire you will need to muster and develop. It must become a need, not just a want. It needs to become a definite goal, not just a wish or a hope.

We will be discussing how desire can become reality in subsequent sections. Suffice it to say that if you have within you a strong, burning desire to achieve a goal, whether it be a large quantity of money, or a personal trait you want to acquire, your engine is started and warmed up, you are moving forward, and you are ready to shift into second.

Everything you do begins with desire, from putting on your pants to being the president of the United States. If you can name something you want or desire, you have within yourself the ability to achieve it. It's the law. Although I can't explain why, it is nevertheless a true principle. If you learn nothing else from this section, learn that it is a natural law. *If you have the desire, you can achieve it.*

Second Gear: Belief

Second gear is *belief.* To believe that you can do it, that it is possible, is equal in importance to your desire. A person won't work on a goal without desire. Likewise, a person won't work on a goal without believing that it is achievable. Belief motivates you to success.

Belief Needs Nurturing

Unlike desire, which seems to appear in our minds automatically, belief needs nurturing. Doubts have a way of creeping in, along with all the negative vibes we receive from others, often including our close friends and family. Because you need to nurture your faith, to believe in yourself, you need to have an understanding of how to build your self-confidence. This gear is like all the other gears. If it is not used, your achievement momentum will be stopped. You will not make it into third gear, much less full speed ahead. People simply won't work toward a goal when their minds are full of all the reasons why they can't do it.

The Three Sources of Faith

There seem to be three sources for developing the faith in yourself necessary to accomplish anything. A discussion of those three important sources follows.

Source #1: Investigation. The first way to develop belief in yourself and in the goal you have is to look into all aspects of it. See if it can be done. Have other people done it? I like to think that no matter what the goal, if other people have done it, you can too.

For instance, if your goal is to earn a large amount of money, say a million dollars, by age forty-five, you may want to look around and see if it has been done before, and by whom. Chances are, you will feel confident when you find out that most of the people who have done it before you were not as educated, not as smart, didn't work as hard, and didn't want it as badly as you do. Chances are, your abilities are already in the top twenty percent of those who are doing it now. You may want to talk to some of those who have accomplished the same goals you have made for yourself. They can tell you some of the pitfalls to look for along the way and how to do certain things to insure success in your goal.

Beware of the Negative

Beware of advice from people who tend to discourage rather than build you up. Unless they have experienced success in your area before, they may not understand the power of your desires. They may not think you can or should do it. They probably give discouraging advice to everybody. Be careful about whom you talk to in your investigation. Only seek out people who seem positive and willing to share their experiences of success with you. Stay away from people with negative ideas and thoughts. If they are the type that like to see success in others, you are probably okay. Positive thoughts seem to need more nurturing, more effort to develop. Negative thoughts flow freely, especially from people who are around you a lot. You must learn to cast out those thoughts.

Many business advisors, whether paid consultants or sources of free counseling from government or volunteer organizations, actually discourage more than they encourage. Often, retired business people can sound negative about your ideas. Some people who have never been in business on their own take pride in discouraging people from doing something they know nothing about themselves. Be careful about whose advice you take. Talk to those who are doing it or who have done it, who have no other stake in what they are telling you, except to give you the straight story about what you want to do. Naturally, some of the people who could give you the most useful advice would be the ones you would be competing against if you went into business for yourself. If you have to go to sources from out of town, so be it. But talk to successful people in your field of endeavor. Most people who are successful like to help others who look up to them, especially those who are interested in doing the same thing they do. They will almost always give you good advice.

Source #2: Visualize. My mother used to tell me that if I wanted to be a good student, I should look and act like one. All my life she has told me I can do anything I want to. It is an advantage if you can have that type of people around you, especially when you are growing up.

Some people don't find it easy to see themselves in a positive way. They can't visualize themselves already in possession of their goal. To many people, success is something for others, something they can't achieve. If you are one of those people, it is very important that you start now visualizing what it is you want and seeing yourself achieving that goal. If you want to be a good student, look around at the other good students. See what they do and begin to see yourself as they are, doing what they do and getting the results they do.

If you want to make a million dollars or own your own business, you need to visualize yourself having the million dollars or running the business. You know that you should always begin with the end in mind. Take that literally. Start now. Begin working toward your goal with the result, or end, in mind. And remember:

> If you think you are beaten, you are,
> If you think you dare not, you don't.
> If you like to win, but you think you can't,
> It is almost certain you won't.
>
> If you think you'll lose, you're lost,
> For out in the world we find,
> Success begins with a fellow's will—
> It's all in the state of mind.
>
> If you think you are outclassed, you are,
> You've got to think high to rise,
> You've got to be sure of yourself before
> You can ever win a prize.
>
> Life's battles don't always go
> To the stronger or faster man,
> But soon or late the man who wins
> Is the man *who thinks he can!*
>> (author unknown, quoted in *Think and Grow Rich* by Napoleon Hill)

Every good coach or athlete can tell you about the importance of self-visualization. They have to see where they are going each season, where they are going to end up. They must see success the whole time they are preparing for the first game, and all other games along the way.

All good successful athletes and coaches will tell you that visualizing results helps to achieve those results.

If you are constantly visualizing yourself losing the game or failing to achieve the goal you desire, you will most certainly lose. Most people will tell you that while negative thoughts and visualizations come into your mind automatically, positive, winning results have to be placed there. Later we will discuss the value of reviewing your goals daily. Suffice it to say here that if you spend some time each day concentrating on your goal's positive results, you will be miles ahead.

Source #3: Try it. The best way to build faith in your ability to accomplish something is to do it. Confidence will come from positive experiences. You can study and visualize an idea all year long, but until you try it—get some practical experiences, take some steps—you will really never know what you can do.

"I Wish I Had Done It Earlier"

Ask almost anyone you know who has a successful business how they felt when they started. They will probably say they were scared and somewhat doubtful. Then ask how they feel now. I'm sure they now feel confident that they could do almost anything. In fact, most of them will say that they wish they had done it earlier. And why didn't they? Usually they just hadn't developed enough confidence or faith in themselves to do it.

Investigate your goal through good, reliable sources. Keep a positive attitude about it. Constantly visualize yourself successfully achieving your goal. Get started now by giving it a try. Even if it is a slow, careful start, you will begin to develop the confidence you need to carry on. If you have the desire to achieve your goal and believe that you can do it, you are ready to shift into third.

Third Gear: Decision

Decision is the beginning of action. You may have successfully gone through the process to this point, but the real evidence that the process will be completed is the decision to act and the decision to stick with it until it is accomplished. You may want something and believe that you can achieve it, but to make the decision to act is the real, substantive evidence that it is about to happen.

Decision Makers

The inability to make decisions is a major factor in many unfulfilled goals. You get stuck in second and can't get going. This is one of the major reasons that people use only two to five percent of their natural ability. What a waste of a human resource.

Successful people are usually quick decision makers. And their decisions are seldom changed. They know where they are going—they have a plan. They make the decision to go there, and they don't stop until they get there. They aren't swayed by other people's negative opinions and input. They make their decisions on their own, after thorough research and investigation, proving what they can do with their decisions and actions rather than their words. They see a good idea and they go for it, never looking back until they are there. A good idea doesn't get any better with time. The person who procrastinates the decision to act allows time for doubt, indecision, and fear to enter into the picture, delaying the action. This increases the chances of halting the process altogether.

Listen and Decide

Many people like to talk to everyone they know about their ideas. The best advice is to be quiet about your good ideas. Don't talk too much about what you are going to do. Practice sitting back and listening more than talking all about what you are doing and what your plan is. You should only talk about your ideas and plans to people from whom you are seeking advice on the subject. And be careful who they are. The longer you talk and solicit advice about it, the longer you are putting off acting on the idea. Before long, someone else may be doing it. Negative thoughts may have crept into your mind, or doubt may have taken away your desire to act.

Decision is another one of those silent steps that many people never learn to take. To some people it comes naturally, to others it's difficult, and a few people find it all but impossible. It is clear that a person never gets any farther than second gear without making that all-important decision to act by shifting into third. And second gear won't get you very far.

Fourth Gear: Plan

Stephen R. Covey once said, "To begin with the end in mind means to start with a clear understanding of your destination." Fourth gear is your *plan*. I went to see an attorney many years ago to set up a business organization. We were forming a land development limited partnership. One suggestion the seasoned business attorney made to me was to begin with the end in mind. He then asked, "Where do you want to be with this project many years from now? Do you want to sell the project immediately or keep it? What is your plan?"

Everyone Knows How to Do It

Here is another one of those steps everyone uses every day to do virtually everything. They make a plan. Everyone knows how to do it. Everyone does it all day long, usually without even being aware of it. Most people never think about planning—they just do it. Getting up from your desk and making your way to the drinking fountain down the hall requires a plan. Driving home and eating dinner is planned. We don't realize that we make a plan first because many things we do are so basic and habitual. Everything you do, from the smallest function to the long-range, lifelong goal, has a plan. You may not realize it, but you have a plan for everything. You couldn't name anything that doesn't have a plan. You should understand that you are already good at planning, because you do it every day for everything you do. Once you understand that, you can use the same system for achieving your more meaningful goals and missions.

The Blueprint

I used to be in the land development business. Before I would even think about constructing a building on a piece of property—in fact, before I would even close the purchase on the lot—I would have a site plan prepared by an architect. I would submit that plan to all the necessary branches of the local government to see if the building would fit on the lot and if the local building codes were met for my design. A grading plan would be submitted to the engineering department so they would know we had proper water drainage and so I would know if I had to do much cutting and filling of dirt. All of this can get very expensive, but it's nice to know about what your expenses are going to be before you buy the lot. Just think what would happen if you didn't check all those things out beforehand. You would buy the lot, only to find out that you can't put anything on it that makes sense, let alone any profit.

Why You Will Not Become President

You may begin to understand why some people never work toward becoming the president of the United States, or even some other goal such as starting a business of their own. They understand the process of a plan in everything they do, but they fail to use the same process to accomplish some of their strongest desires in life.

Why, then, do so many people dream of doing something like starting their own business, acquire the necessary self-confidence, and then drop the idea and never proceed? Have you ever seen anyone going down the street in second gear with the engine racing? You probably said, "Why don't they shift that thing?"

This Is Where Things Get Dropped

Most people don't achieve their goals because they forget about them. They get an idea, get pumped up about it, talk like they want to do it, and sometimes even make up a plan for its achievement. Sometimes they even put the plan on paper in detail. Then what happens?

Have you ever set a goal to lose weight beginning January first? What happened? Chances are, if you are like me and everyone else, you forgot about it. You didn't think about it each morning, recommit to do it, and picture yourself thin. You didn't have a plan, or you didn't follow it.

We Do What We Are Thinking about at the Time

The reason that people don't continue on into fifth gear toward the successful achievement of their goals is that they don't set up in a formal plan in a detailed, written form that they can review each day.

We work on what we are thinking about. That is why many successful people use planners or calendars. If you don't plan where you are going each day, a lot of time can be wasted. Almost all students of time management agree that it is wise to work priorities on a daily basis. And many people are good at it. Have you ever seen people carrying their planners into restaurants? Then, when they get up to go to the bathroom, they take it with them, don't they?

Some people are organized to a fault. They plan and execute with excellence on a daily basis. But many of them never learn that the way you accomplish a long-range goal is to use the same process that they use every day for the little things, only in a long-range manner.

Use Short-Term Methods to Achieve Long-Term Goals

The planning area of the success process is treated in more books and seminars than any of the other steps. But it can be simple if you want it to be. One of the goals of this book is to convince you of how uncomplicated it is. Consider the following simple system for making your plan and following it. You can read thousands of pages on this subject and spend lots of money on seminars. Save the time and money. They all end up saying, in many different and complicated ways, that you need to capture your goals in writing and remind yourself of them daily. If you don't remind yourself, you won't work on them. If you don't work on them, they won't happen.

The Three Principles of Planning Follow-Up

Principle #1: Write down each specific step of your plan. Write down on a piece of paper exactly what you want to achieve. Be very specific, naming exactly the amount of money you want, the kind of business you intend to establish, the personality trait you want to develop, or the relationship you want to nurture. Whatever it is you want, write it down.

Principle #2: Write out a milestone schedule and the date for final accomplishment of your goal. Write a schedule of your intended accomplishments with dates of when each step is to be achieved and the final date when you want to have the goal reached. This will establish checkpoints for you to push yourself along a specific plan or trail toward your major goal.

Principle #3: Review it every day. Keep it with you always, and establish the habit of referring to it at least twice daily. I would particularly recommend that one of those times be in the morning before you head out for your busy day. It is good to memorize it, but always go over it with concentration at least twice daily.

It Must Remain a Priority

If you do not go to at least that much trouble to formalize the plan and commit to stay with the daily reminder and commitment, you are going to forget the goal. Even if you do remember it, it will not be a priority in your daily schedule.

When my mother told me to look and act like a good student if I wanted to become one, I didn't realize the depth of that lesson. If you have a desire, set the goal by writing it down, think about it every day, and begin to see, act, and think as if you have already successfully reached your goal. You will be well on your way to achieving it.

People who have achieved their goals—by first desiring to accomplish them and then deciding to do act on them—will tell you that the three principles of planning follow-up are a minimum in the process of success. Planning and reviewing the plan regularly will help you keep the end in mind. If you don't have the end in mind all along the way, it follows that you will not work toward the goal on a daily basis. Write specific goals and objectives, list the dates for accomplishment, and then review them at least twice daily. That is the process in a nutshell.

Virtually everyone knows the process from their experience with everyday living, but they fail to use that experience to accomplish their long-term goals. Many people have good ideas that are useless because they do not act upon them. And why do they fail to act on them? It is usually simply because they forget their ideas by not writing them down, much less committing to review them daily. If you write them down and review them daily you will not forget them. Remember, you only do what you are thinking about, what you want, and what you believe you can do.

Fifth Gear: Action

Fifth gear in the process of success is *action*. Ideas are useless until they are acted upon. This is the fun stage of the process of success. Most of the big steps are behind you. It is here that exciting things happen along the road to achieving important goals.

You Are on the Road

You have now devised a specific written plan for achieving your goal which has incorporated within it a method for daily self-reminder. If you have not gotten that far yet, put a book marker right here, set this book down, and write out your plan to accomplish your desire before you do anything else. Refer back to the plan section for review and help. Remember, the plan doesn't have to be long and difficult. You can type it up on your computer later, and you can revise it and formalize it later also. Just write out your plan roughly and begin now to implement it. You are now ready to glide along the freeway in fifth gear, enjoying exciting experiences along the way.

Do You Have to Work Hard?

It's time to use that dirty four-letter word: work. The role of work in success is often misunderstood. Some people say that the harder you work, the more money you will make. Others say that it is a God-given principle and we must work hard and teach our children to work hard. They say, "When the going gets tough, the tough get going." Parents want their children to learn to work, and by that they often really mean they want them to have the security of a good job.

Some people have asked why work is not one of the steps to success. The fact is, it is. Most people who find success in life have to work hard to get there. But it is not one of the gears; it is not an essential element of the process. Many successful people work only a few hours at what is creating most of their income. They probably worked hard during the creation stage, but many of their businesses are now operating just fine, so they can play golf or run some other venture to raise their leverage level and create even more income. Many hard-working folks who were properly taught throughout their lives never make more than a living with their labors. Most people spend their entire lives trying to make a living and fail to direct any efforts toward trying to make some money!

Harder or Smarter

You have probably heard the advice to work smarter, not harder. Many people have heard it, but few understand it. The man who learns to work smarter rather than harder is the guy who is leveraging his time and talents. How many hours one puts in at work has about as much to do with his success as how much he sweats.

Lest you think that you don't have to work hard to be successful, be assured you that most successful people work very hard at getting where they are. When I worked for a corporation briefly when I was just out of college, I could hardly stand to work eight hours. But when I started my own business, I enjoyed working for myself so much more that I worked more than eight hours quite often. The actual work I did for the corporation was more interesting and challenging. I negotiated with attorneys and dealt with the public. In my own business the work was usually more mundane or routine. But it was mine. All the money was going to me. It became more fun to work hard.

There are two sides to work. You can spend too much time working hard and getting nowhere. That is why you call showing up at your job "going to work." That's what you do—you work. You don't move forward. You don't advance. You just work. That makes parents and grandparents happy. But it may not make *you* happy. Consider how it would be if your work efforts were going to build equity in *your* business instead of your boss's.

"There's No Free Lunch"

If you are going to go into business for yourself, you had better prepare to work hard, especially at first. You've heard that there's no free lunch. Your work may not be the same as if you were an employee. You will be training, planning, following up on employees, worrying about finances, and interpreting financial statements. Those duties may not seem like work to the guy who has been working for others all his life, but they are work. Let's call it running your business, if you like, and let your employees call it work. Whatever you want to call it, you will be working just as hard or harder to be successful in your own business.

Persistence

The driving force, or staying power, behind action is persistence. Humans seem to get bored easily. They get tired of things after a while. With some people, it's five years. They call themselves a five-year people. They like change and new challenges, and after about five years they seem to start looking for new challenges. Whatever it is, boredom, bad feedback, financial or other setbacks, or being a five-year kind of guy, often people don't stick with what they are trying to accomplish.

You might be wise to stipulate as one of your goals or objectives never to give up. Be determined to make it. Be persistent until you are there. You want it, you know it can be done, and you have a plan. Now just stay at it until you get it, no matter what or how long it takes. Consider the words of Calvin Coolidge:

> Nothing can take the place of persistence. Talent will not; nothing is more common than unsuccessful people with talent. Genius will not; unrewarded genius is almost a proverb. Education will not; the world is full of educated derelicts. Persistence and determination alone are the omnipotent.

Remember, most successful people go through some tough times and even failures along the way. But they always seem to get there. It's not easy to be persistent during tough times. But those who stay at it for a long time eventually get there. You can too.

Time Management

If you are going to work hard at this goal of yours, you might just as well be working smart with the time you will be investing. If you don't develop the ability to manage your time, you may be spinning your wheels. It will certainly take longer to get there.

There are entire books and seminars devoted to time management. You should study up on it. A lot of time is lost doing things that don't mean anything to people's progress and goals. Study the subject and organize yourself toward accomplishing your most important missions and objectives. Spend your valuable time doing what matters most, what will produce the best results in the minimum amount of time. Work priorities. There is family, community, and work. And in your work, there are important things to do that produce the most results, and there are unimportant things to do that waste your time. You will learn that time management is really priority management, that you must say no to certain activities that matter least and yes to the activities that matter most to the accomplishment of your mission and goals.

Keep to the Plan

Successful people are a minority. Most people not only don't reach their goals, but they don't set them high enough either. They fail to reach their human potential. But success is available to everyone, and it is not difficult or complicated. It can be predicted and calculated with mathematical accuracy. You just have to work your plan on a daily basis to the best of your ability. If you miss a day, you shouldn't quit, lose interest, or radically change the plan. You should get right back to the plan the next day and do your best to stay on track from then on. If a plan needs changing, change it. But keep advancing. If it was a good idea back when you devised the plan, it is a good idea now. Keep to it.

Be a People Watcher

Watch others who are successful in your field. You can learn a lot that way. You may see some things being done that you should incorporate into your plan. Successful people are not hard to find. Find someone who enjoys the success you desire, and don't be afraid to ask questions and learn from his or her example. Most successful people like to help. Don't be afraid to ask.

Take "Luck" Out of Your Vocabulary

Many people still think success is luck or getting the breaks, as if by chance. They don't understand that success is following simple steps on a day-to-day basis and not giving up until the plan has been fully achieved. Success is a process. Thomas Edison once said, "I never did anything worth doing by accident, nor did any of my inventions come by accident." Sure, some people get breaks, and some people are occasionally lucky. But closely examine each case and you will conclude that those breaks were created or invited with a plan in the action stage.

An Example of "Luck"

In my case, I had started my little service business in southern California. I set goals yearly and I had an overall goal I was working toward. I went along for twelve years with slight growth each year, slowly bettering the previous year but not breaking any records. As I look back, I realize that my goals were quite modest. I should have set them much higher.

All of a sudden I received an invitation to visit a friend of mine at his office, where he was the CEO of a large, well-known restaurant chain. I had known him for some years and had been pounding at him for some business for most of those years. His company could have used my services all along. Any kind of an order from a company that size would have been a boost to a little firm like mine. But there were just too many people between him and those who made the decisions to hire firms like mine. Sometimes even knowing the CEO can't make certain things happen for you.

I had known him for twelve years and had been running my little business for the same length of time. Then I received the invitation to visit his office. We chatted about a way my little company could be of service to his billion-dollar corporation. I walked out with an order to do some investigative services amounting to about a 23% increase in my gross income. I was happy.

That nice little order became a 28% increase, and then 71%. It eventually led to a visit with their operations people, who asked for a proposal for what would increase my business by 471%. The proposal was accepted, and I was elated. It was a real break for me. I was happy that I knew the CEO. Was I lucky?

I started my little business from scratch, with very little capital, no office, used machines, and a Volkswagen Beetle. I followed a plan, the same as described above. I was gliding along in fifth gear, putting that plan into action. I developed the business, cultivated relationships, and attempted to put the sales touch on all possible associates and friends. I made myself visible. When my CEO friend needed the kind of service I had to offer, I was the one he knew that was doing it. He knew me. He trusted me. He knew my abilities. I was there. I was in the right place at the right time. That is not luck. I started the business. I knew my business. I was good at what I did. I was licensed and bonded to do it. And I worked on him for twelve years. I earned it. It was not a lucky break, it was a nice break. You don't work for something for twelve years and call it lucky. It would have been luck if I had gotten that order my first day in business.

Luck is all of a sudden one day receiving a large sum of money from an unknown relative who just died. Luck is winning the lottery. Some people say that's the best way to make it. But don't hold your breath. A break is created or earned by being there, trained and ready, with the service or product that is needed by someone prepared to pay for it. Being born rich, being lucky, or being crooked is not success. The sooner you get that fallacy out of your thinking, the faster you will get there. The steps to success are easy to understand and easy to follow. It is almost mechanical. It is not new or mysterious. It is open for all to know. It is a natural law that will reward you. Napoleon Hill once said, "Fortunate is the person who has developed the self-control to steer a straight course toward his objective."

The action part of the personal success process is all downhill and fun. This is when you experience the excitement of success as you work toward the fulfillment of your goals. You experience what it is like to accomplish something that you decide to do yourself rather than doing something that someone else told you to do.

Learning to work smarter rather than harder is a good feeling. It makes you feel smart, fulfilled, and self-confident. Remember, it does take work to accomplish anything worthwhile. There is no free lunch.

Put forth the effort to learn how to manage your time. Much time is wasted in life. Learn to work the priorities so you are spending your time on the things that matter most. Identify people you look up to because they accomplish their goals. Watch them for ideas on how to be more like them.

Remove the word *luck* from your vocabulary. Realize that success and accomplishment is a process with certain steps to follow. Everyone follows them daily, but most people fail to use that same process to go after their dreams. If you can get dressed every day, you can act to successfully accomplish any of your desires.

Reverse Gear: Fear

Fear is the reverse gear in the process of personal achievement. It is the reason people go backwards—away from their goals—instead of forward. Napoleon Hill once said, "Fears are nothing more than states of mind. One's state of mind is subject to control and direction." You are in control of the gears you use. You can choose to go forward or backward.

The Fear of Something

We have talked about how to cultivate a belief in yourself, how to make a decision to go forward, how to make a personal plan, and how to act on that plan. Fear is the biggest stumbling block to achieving success with your plan.

We also talked about how some people spend most of their time making a living but never devote any of their time toward making money. I believe these people fear change, criticism, and failure. They are, for the moment, doing okay in their jobs. They make a living. They are doing what family, parents, grandparents, friends, and associates think they should do. Why change? It could mean disaster and poverty. People will criticize, making those well-meaning remarks that set you back a notch. If what you set out to do fails, then there are the I-told-you-so's.

It's no wonder people fear failure. It can be devastating. Most of us who have been in the business world for any length of time have experienced some sort of setback. You are down and out. You feel naked and exposed. Setting a goal such as starting a new business and quitting your job opens up the opportunity for failure. That possibility can cause a person to put it off or decide not to do it at all. But you never hear people say they are afraid. People will say, "Hey, I'm going to go into business for myself." Then, six months later you ask them how it's going. They say they have put it on the back burner for a while, citing every reason in the book except that they are afraid they will fail and have to face the world with that fact. So their project gets put off or dropped altogether. Or they progress so slowly, being so overcautious, that the project just never gets done.

Courage versus Fear

It does take guts to start your own business or to do something out of the ordinary to get ahead. Most people don't recognize that they are silently respected by others for doing things out of the ordinary, for taking risks to get ahead. Even though you have heard entrepreneurs defined as those who take risks, entrepreneurs will tell you differently. They consider it a common fallacy. They are really risk avoiders. They don't look at a business start-up as a risk. It is an opportunity.

Entrepreneurs are respected. We all know entrepreneurs who have started many different businesses through the years. Most of them have lost some of the enterprises, but they still operate one or more of the successful ones. Entrepreneurs don't pay any attention to the negative criticism.

How to Fight This Enemy

1. Reject negative input. First, you must learn to block negative input out of your mind. Well-meaning people will sometimes, in subtle ways, direct negative opinions and criticism toward you. This kind of criticism is particularly damaging, because it often comes from those you respect. Remember, you must be the captain of your ship. Do your own thinking and direct your own plan. You are the boss. Even those whom you consider to be qualified to give you counsel may give negative comments, because they may not understand the process themselves.

I have had many people ask me my opinion about their ideas for a business or their desire to go into some profession. Often I think they must be crazy. Sometimes I don't believe they will be successful. But I bite my tongue and discuss the pluses and minuses of such a business without giving my opinion. I don't like to discourage people with negative thoughts. They may just make it even though I couldn't, or they may want to be something I don't.

The experts will tell you that negative influences enter the mind with ease, but that positive thoughts have to be placed there. Learn that you are in control of what goes into your subconscious mind. It is a matter of willpower. When someone makes a negative comment about a book

I am writing or a business I'm thinking about starting, I immediately say to myself, "That is one comment I must disregard." I try to forget that I heard it.

2. Keep the proper company. Second, try to associate with people who think like you do, who are not negative. You can control better what goes into your mind by cutting off some of the sources of the criticism and negativity. I tell my teenagers that they will do what the people they associate with do. I try to encourage them to be around good people for that reason. You do the same. Associate with people who will allow you the latitude to do your own thinking and execute your own plans without criticism.

3. Be positive. Third, develop a positive attitude. If someone shoots a negative comment at you, shoot right back. Interrupt their sentence with a comment that lets them know that you don't welcome their negativism and that you are moving ahead despite them. Or change the subject quickly. It is good to keep a positive mental attitude. Shut out the negative and let the positive in. Some people even suggest that you shouldn't talk about your project at all. If nobody knows about it, they can't comment. Do what makes you most comfortable. But when you are around people who insist on talking negatively about your project, realize that they are probably just jealous or afraid.

4. Act now—never look back. Fourth, act now, and continue acting on your plan. "He who hesitates is lost." Don't let delays creep into your plan schedule. Stay on schedule. Don't ask for too much input. You be the judge. Trust your own judgment on how the plan is going. Start now if you haven't started yet, and move on to your destination. There will be no time for fear and doubt to slow you down.

5. Perform well. Fifth, go for quality and do your best. This will give you confidence in your project or goal. It will leave less room for unwanted criticism.

In Summary

In this chapter we have discussed the need to be organized and on track personally before you can expect to succeed at a business of your own. If you have the desire, you also have the ability to achieve it. You just have to believe, make the decision, write out a plan, and act.

Remember, no one can think for you. Control your own thoughts. Fear will try to creep into your mind either by itself or through others. Develop ways to keep it out. Be your own boss. Be decisive. Be the leader. If you have to listen to negative input from a close friend or family member, then quickly disregard it and stay with your plan. Keep so busy doing it that there isn't time to be afraid.

And by all means, don't think you are alone. Everyone who ever did anything worthwhile felt some fears trying to accomplish their plan. They overcame the problem and succeeded. You can too.

Part 2

The Seven Practices of Enduring Businesses

If you were to ask me what I thought it really took to be successful in a small business in the 1990s, this would be my answer to you.

Chapter 4

Practice One: Put People First

The Practice of Treating People Well

Industries of the future will not depend on physical "hardware," which can be duplicated anywhere, but on the human "software," which can retain a technological edge.

Robert B. Reich, *The Next American Frontier*

The Golden Rule

Some people think that the golden rule means "he who has the gold rules." I have heard some real horror stories about how people are treated, both as employees and as customers. It appears that business owners and managers have not yet learned a very important, centuries-old business principle: the focus of business leaders must first be on treating people well, employees as well as customers, and then on profits.

This is not meant to be a Sunday School lesson, because the golden rule is an important business principle as well. It translates into solid bottom-line profits. Edwin Markham said, "We have committed the golden rule to memory; let us now commit it to life."

Unfortunately, the focus of many business leaders is that bottom line. They are in business to create profits. They haven't yet learned that by focusing on people first, the bottom line will fall into place naturally.

Caveat Emptor

There is a legal term, *caveat emptor*, that means "let the buyer beware." It summarizes the rule that a purchaser must examine, judge, and test for himself the product he is purchasing. It is not fraud to "puff your wares" by putting your best foot forward in advertising, by bragging up your product or service. But people are getting tired of product and service providers placing the onus on customers to be careful about what they buy. People want the provider to be careful. They want the provider to bear part of that burden. Customers want it to be easy and pleasant. Customers don't want to beware. They want the provider to beware. Nevertheless, the seller may not be telling the buyer all the true facts about the product or service in the "puffed" advertising. Buyers should understand that the seller is trying to sell his wares and make a profit. In so doing, the seller may not be telling the whole truth.

I don't know about you, but I don't like shopping. When I go out to look for something I need, or when I need something done by a service firm, I like to know I'm going to get what I bargained for and I don't like to have to hire a private investigator to check everything out. I go to places I know already have fair treatment policies in place. If I sense that they are more concerned about their profits on my deal rather than getting me back into their place for future business, I go somewhere else.

Caveat Venditor

There is another *caveat* legal term that is not used much. *Caveat venditor* means "let the seller beware." While you don't hear the term much these days, the "seller beware" policy of treating people right is creeping back into free-world business here in the 1990s. More businesses accept returned merchandise without argument, which is what they used to do. Businesses are treating people better and are paying more attention to them. And this gradual movement toward reasonable service is causing welcome competition. We will discuss this subject in detail later, but suffice it to say for now that enduring businesses are coming around to the fact that people, both employees and customers, truly are the most valuable assets of a company. While employees are not actually accounted for on the asset column of the balance sheet, their efforts are clearly reflected in the income statement under "net income."

"Our Employees Are Our Greatest Asset"

In addition to the improved treatment customers are getting, we also hear stories of owners and managers who say "our employees are our greatest asset." Nevertheless, we all know where employees are found in company financial statements, and it's not under "assets." They are expenses, found on the income statement as a deduction against revenues to find bottom-line profits. Because of this fact, many owners and managers treat them as expenses, to be cut where possible, to be obtained by paying only what the market will bear, and to be disposed of at will.

As for where customers are on the financial statements, you might argue a place for them on the balance sheet, in the asset column under "goodwill." Owners often treat customers with more respect than employees for that reason. They see customers as an asset, but employees as expenses.

Profits, People, or Both?

Most business literature rejects the view that the sole function of business should be profit making. They discuss other business motives such as providing meaningful work, producing goods and services for society, or correcting social problems. Each business owner must decide which motive or combination of motives is most important for his business. But for the purposes of the subject at hand, we must reject the idea that profit making is the sole function of a business. Those who feel that profit making alone naturally solves all of our social and economic ills need to take another look at the evidence.

When firms concentrate only on the bottom line, problems such as pollution (air, water, and noise) and unemployment creep up. No one claims that firms should employ for the sake of employment at the expense of profits. We all know profits are vital. The problem is when profit-seeking firms unjustly treat their people like other assets such as equipment, machines, or land.

The firm that makes maximizing profits its sole function often causes problems for society and suffering for its owners. Companies need to learn that they can and must concentrate on both. There is nothing wrong with a goal to make profits, but it is a crucial mistake to treat people as assets or land and not to consider them uniquely worthy of respect. Profits suffer when companies focus heavily on sales and the promotion of products and don't spend sufficient time, energy, and funds on employees. Human assets solve problems, deal with customers, and otherwise produce value. When employees are not happy and being treated well, they don't produce profits as well.

Beware, sellers! The attitudes and skills that make people happier, healthier, and more cooperative human beings are the same attitudes and skills that make people more productive. By promoting a "people-first" attitude, you just may be promoting your profits as well.

Wherever they put people on the balance sheet, as assets or expenses, owners had better begin thinking of people as people, not equipment. A piece of equipment must be used to its maximum productivity. It must be purchased for the lowest possible price, and when it fails to continue to produce properly, it is discarded, often for scrap.

Some owners handle their people just like equipment and wonder why their employees treat their customers the same way. People are a means to an end to them. They consider their employees to be their property, like their equipment, and they want them to produce or get out. That is the message they send to their employees, and the employees receive it, loud and clear. Unfortunately, that feeling is also reflected in the service they give to customers.

Authoritarian Leadership

I don't really have any personal horror stories to tell about being treated poorly by my employers as I was growing up. But, if my experience in counseling entrepreneurs and listening to my working teenage children is representative, it appears that there are still plenty of problems in the work force.

My son just left a job washing dishes at a restaurant. He is sixteen years old, and this was just the second job he has ever had. He left his first job thinking that this one would be better. His new supervisor was probably a retired army drill sergeant, because he liked to shout commands using authoritative, rather than persuasive, leadership skills. Authoritarian leadership has its place in the military, but not with any employee in any workplace. My son's last night on the job started when he walked in the door five minutes late. He is usually a punctual kid and was seldom late. For the rest of the night the sergeant yelled at him with language that included the very worst of four-letter words. Most people put their swear words in between other words in a sentence, but this guy was using swear words between syllables! My son walked out and never returned, and I don't blame him. Incidentally, the restaurant isn't doing all that well. Do you wonder why?

Being Unreasonable

Another son worked in a car wash. They scheduled him to work on Saturdays but when he got to work and there were no cars for a time, they would ask him to clock out. He might spend four hours there, but only get paid for two. They also asked him to come to meetings during the week where all employees received instruction. The meetings were mandatory. They were not paid for this time. Guess what? The car wash is not doing well. The one down the street, while charging more for their washes, does much better. Cars are lined up every day for washes, the employees all wear the same colored T-shirts, they all seem to cooperate and work together, and more importantly, they seem happy with their jobs.

Your Number-One Priority

Such treatment of employees, not to mention similar treatment of customers, has long been a common business mistake which can cost firms their growth and often causes their failure. The unfair, demeaning, and domineering treatment of people in any area of life, including in families, is wrong. And it is counterproductive as well. Anyone considering an entrepreneurial venture must learn this lesson in order to succeed. People are your best assets. Employees are the ones who provide customers with your product or service, and customers are the ones who hand you money for that product or service. They are people, just like you. They should be your number-one priority. They should all be happy, content, secure, and well treated. If they are treated fairly, they will treat your customers well, even when you are not around. When you focus on the people in your business, your people will focus on your bottom line for you.

For you who are starting your businesses now, implement a "people-first" program and develop a people-oriented culture. For you who already have businesses going and feel you may have some room for improvement here, begin now to develop a spirit of cooperation, friendship, hard work, and determination to succeed with your people. When you implement such a program, keeping people first, your bottom line profits will fall into place naturally.

Customers Are People Too

Don't you hate it when you go into a store and have to negotiate, argue, and undergo interrogation before buying something? You get the feeling they have different deals for different people. Shopping should be made easy for people. Prices should be set fairly, and service should be given fairly and evenly. Make it comfortable and peaceful, and don't make customers work to shop in your store, or they will go on to the next place.

A Win-Win Attitude

There is a well-discussed theory for the practice of interpersonal relationships circulating at this time. It is called *win-win*. It refers to the attitude that in your dealings with people, you should consider the benefit to the other party with whom you are dealing. You want the dealing solution, an agreement to benefit yourself and the other person. Most think *win-lose*, where you win and the other guy loses. Poor negotiators think *lose-win* and come out short on the deal, because they are weaker negotiators than their counterparts. Selfish, unfair negotiators think win-lose. They always are thinking of themselves at the expense of others.

Win-win is an attitude carried by those who think of more than just the bottom line. It's an attitude that gives people the feeling that they have made a good deal. It's an attitude that keeps people happy and coming back. It's not a sign that the business owner is weak. Rather, it shows strength and wisdom. It's good business sense. Remember, win-win means the owner makes a fair profit too.

Keep in mind that you are looking for lasting, enduring business success and growth. If you temporarily win in a particular deal, you may end up losing in the long run when the customer recognizes that he lost and that you are only in it for the win. Both must win for a long-term relationship to develop.

Put Yourself in Their Shoes

In your desire to learn how to treat people better so your business will endure, cultivate the quality of empathy. Empathy is the ability to place yourself in another's shoes, to understand and almost experience their feelings. Too many of us, in our quest to sell or negotiate or "win," seem to want only to do the talking and to manipulate. Those who learn to listen with the intent to understand the needs and problems of the client, customer, or employees, find better success when they convey the attitude and feeling that they are straightforward and fair. When you understand people's fears and worries, you can then respond with solutions. You should know that much is said in the current business literature about the importance of listening to your customers and clients so that you can better understand their needs. After all, it is their needs that you are trying to meet.

Along with being empathetic to others, it is important to be open and sensitive to suggestions and criticisms. Be humble, easy to work with, and willing to listen, and you will find barriers broken that otherwise would stifle your ability to deal with people.

Employees before Customers?

Hal F. Rosenbluth, of Rosenbluth Inc., an enduring travel agency in the United States, claims that companies must put their employees first. The title of his book, which describes incredible growth and success in a service business, is *The Customer Comes Second*. How many times have we heard that customers come first, and that they are always right?

It Really Does Work

In running your own business, you must learn the importance of treating employees fairly, and it is a principle you must practice consistently. It really does work. It really is serious business philosophy. When you create a positive atmosphere in the work place, your employees will be happy, and the happy employees will treat your customers well. And that is the goal.

It is gratifying to note that the Rosenbluth philosophy places profits third on a hierarchical list of concerns in his business. Every company has such a hierarchical list. Theirs is: "People, service, profits," in that order. The company's focus is on its people. The people then focus on serving the clients. Profits are the end result.

"The pillars upon which many companies are built are primarily profit-oriented. We contend these pillars are not strong enough to hold the weight of companies, particularly in lean times. Human beings must be the pillars of a company. They provide an unshakable foundation. This might appear to be a soft strategy but, in our case, we rely on our growth and client retention rates to prove that this method translates into solid results." (p. 39)

Service Businesses Too

The same is true if you have a service business. Customers should get what they bargained for and more. If something isn't right, return and provide it for them. Satisfied customers are now your source of future business. And satisfied customers will tell other potential customers about you. Remember, 80% of the people doing what you are doing have customers who are looking for somebody else to take their place. Most people are looking for another appliance repairman, another plumber they can trust, or a different attorney. If you are performing a service, keep yourself in the 20% area on the spectrum of service so they will refer people to you.

It's Noticeable

There is a large, well-known clothing store near my home that is the perfect example of treating people well. You can tell it is their policy to greet you with a smile, take good care of you from the moment you walk into any department, and help you until you either walk away or say "I'll take it." They have it or they will order it, and they can get any size you need. It is difficult to shop there without being satisfied.

Do you pay more for that kind of service and quality? Yes, that store is more expensive than most. I guess it costs more to give quality and good service. But it also takes good management with a good attitude and happy employees with a desire to do well. It starts at the top with qualified, ambitious executives, and it trickles down to the newest entry-level employees. I'll bet their employees treat the public just the way they are treated by management.

In Summary

The best rule for dealing with people has always been to treat them the way you like to be treated. While most of us have not been formally trained, common sense and your own experience will tell you how to do it. If it felt good when you were treated well, then treat others that same way. Often, that is as much training in how to treat people as the guy with the MBA got.

People don't want to have to be on their guard when they interact with businesses. The seller of goods and services should be aware that people feel this way and that the onus is on him to keep customers happy, content, and coming back.

As for employees, who are certainly people too, it is becoming clear to successful companies and business scholars alike that their people truly are their greatest asset. In fact, some say they should come first, and customers second. This means that they should not be treated merely as something in the asset column of the balance sheet, nor just as an expense on the income statement, but as the producers of the all-important profit. It has clearly been shown that firms that value their employees above profits have employees who create more profits as a result.

People who are running a business, or who want to start one, should develop "people-first" attitudes such as win-win negotiation, empathy, and fairness. When in doubt as to what to do, or how to think, remember the golden rule. It may be the oldest, but it is still the best rule for governing interpersonal relationships.

Chapter 5

Practice Two: Do What You Say

The Practice of Being Dependable and Punctual

Being on time is a value in our culture. . . . Being late is just plain rude and inappropriate.

Jan Yager

The Perfect Example

There was a contractor in my area whom I used for various projects. He was fast and did quality work. His prices were competitive and fair. I always felt confident when he was around that the job would pass the necessary inspections and be done right.

He was an excellent general contractor too. He could coordinate other subcontractors and knew all about the building business. He was good at solving problems created by others, such as the architect. He would say, "No problem, we'll just do it this way. It'll be all right." When he said that, I felt comfortable. I trusted him to get it done, and done right.

On the other hand, he never came when he said he would, and he didn't call to say he wasn't coming. He didn't return calls when I requested, and he seldom finished a job before I had to plead with him to get back to work. Finally, I had to stop using him. I considered him to be a very good contractor, but I couldn't use him anymore, and I couldn't give him a good recommendation.

A Common Frustration

This is a common source of frustration for most people. Those who have been in business for any length of time and have dealt with people who throw your schedule off by showing up late or not at all know what I am talking about. There are certain kinds of businesses (which I won't name here) that have reputations for being flagrant violators of these principles. Some of them end up being the butt of jokes. It's tempting to mention some, but I will resist. Each of us probably has our own ideas about who the worst of the violators are, based on our own experiences in using some of their services.

It's Just Common Sense

I started my little service business based on the principles discussed in this book. To me, they have always been basic, commonsense techniques that last. When I started my business, I chose the name to include a word that reflected the common weakness of the others who were doing the same thing in the area. They were slow, so I put the word "quick" in my company name. I wanted to use the title to get the word out to my potential customers that our principal objective was to provide quick service, because that was the major problem plaguing the industry.

Operations and Scheduling

Maybe it is difficult to operate certain types of services. Product-oriented retail businesses don't seem to suffer as much from poor service. But some services are consistently bad. Maybe it is difficult to coordinate jobs for a contractor or to keep patients running smoothly through a doctor's office. Maintaining a cost-effective operation is important to businesses. But too much emphasis can be placed upon your efficient operation to keep income up. This may cost you customers, clients, or patients, because they will perceive you to be late or undependable. They will also perceive you to be dishonest because you said you would do something that they feel you knew, or should have known, you would never be able to accomplish.

The question of how to schedule properly and perform as promised is a problem faced by many businesses. How efficient can you afford to be and maintain the level of service that keeps the people coming back for more? New businesses face this dilemma. I remember the first little order I received in my business. I took the order myself, and I went out and performed the service myself the same day. The next day I packaged it up more than I needed to and delivered it personally, dropping it off at the front desk so the attorney wouldn't know it was me doing the actual work. New business owners want to take good care of their new clients so they can build the business. Then, when business gets busy, the service sometimes slips. It's hard to keep things even.

Maintaining Your Reputation

I promised myself I would not let this happen to my new little business when I started it. It was in my mission statement and my goals. But it was difficult. The bigger my business got, the more of a problem it became. I constantly had to monitor the level of service I was delivering.

Here are some pointers for maintaining your reputation for dependability, as tough as it may be during times of growth. It is certainly a better problem to have more business than you can handle than not enough. Every business owner prays for this problem. "When it rains, it pours." Never get upset when lots of business comes your way. Just fake it, and figure out a way to get it done.

1. Always Call

Never, never, *never* be late or fail to show up without calling. It may be impossible in your type of business to keep things always on an even keel. Almost everyone who is busy has problems being on time to every appointment. But never be late, and never fail to show up for a promised appointment without calling first. Of the seven practices we are discussing, failure to heed this one will cause the most grief. There is no easier way to create a bad impression, a lack of trust, or an impression of flakiness.

Some people, when marking an appointment in their planners or appointment books, will also take down the phone number of the person they are going to see. This way, they can call if there is a problem. Always ask where they can be reached on the day of the appointment and make a note of it. It's impressive when someone asks that question and marks the phone number down. It says that they want to be prepared if something happens and they can't make it on time. You know they will be calling so you can change your schedule to meet theirs.

Most of us really are understanding and accommodating when someone calls with a problem keeping an appointment. Depending on what the appointment is for, often we are even happy when it is changed. Naturally, we are very irritated when the appointment is missed without any call. I suspect the person missing the appointment could even change it several times without losing the deal. Most of us would work with people forever. A "no problem, just call me and keep me informed" attitude is the one most of us have. But our goodwill only lasts as long as we are kept informed. Learn this one lesson, especially if you have a business where people are depending on you to perform a service, and you will have business coming out of the woodwork.

Begin with this habit, and put it into your mission statement and goals. Make it a commitment. Return all calls promptly, and always call *before* you miss an appointment, not after. Do what you have to to make this your policy. Use a pager, use a cellular phone, or use a pay phone. Mooch off other people's telephones. But *always call.*

2. Learn How to Say No

There is a foreign car auto repair shop I take one of my cars to. The owner is a classic example of the guy who can't say "no." As I write this, my car is sitting over a weekend in his shop. I had to have it towed there last Thursday because it quit running in the middle of the day. When it stalled, I called him and asked if he could get right on it if I had it towed to his shop. He said he would and offered to have his guy pick it up. I agreed. He told me he would at least diagnose it by the end of the day and that I should call before the end of the day.

When I called him at about five o'clock that afternoon, he had not looked at it. He said to call him by ten o'clock the next morning and it would be done. I decided to go by to see if I could figure out why he wasn't doing my job. When I arrived he could hardly talk to me. He was either on the phone or talking to someone who had just pulled in with a car that needed repairing. It was quite obvious. He was too busy.

He had a lot of other cars in his shop that were promised ahead of mine. When he told me he could get right on my job, he knew, or should have known, that it was impossible. What made it worse was that each time I went back on Friday he told me the same thing. He would get right on it, and I should call or come back in a few hours.

I did just what he said. I went back by, each time thinking I would finally find out what was wrong with my car and when I would be able to get it back. My car is dead in the water in his shop today, Saturday, and I still don't know what is wrong or when I will get it back. I wish he had just said no. He is a good mechanic, and I feel confident about his work, but I probably will not use him again because I get too frustrated with his flakiness. If he had said, "No, I won't be able to get to it today, but I can put it in line for a Monday morning diagnosis," I may have been a happy camper today. But now I know that when I go in there in the future, I will not be able to believe what he says.

Human Nature

Most people like saying yes. It's human nature to agree. They don't like to disagree or confront. It is easier to say yes, more difficult and uncomfortable to say no. Some people can't even use the word no. They might be asked if they can do something, and not wanting to use the N-word, they say something else that isn't a strong commitment but sounds like one, like, "I'll do my best," or, "I'll try." The people to whom they are committing accept it as a yes and expect them to show up and perform. When they don't show, they weren't dishonest. They did their best, or they tried. They just didn't do it.

That is why many salesmen are successful. They are using their best sales efforts, being positive and not accepting no for an answer. The fact is, many salesmen don't have to worry about someone saying no. If they just keep talking, they will eventually make the sale, because people like to agree.

It is the same with making commitments such as with my foreign car mechanic friend. Time is lost and reputations are tarnished by not learning how to take control of yourself, be honest, and say, very nicely and gently, no. More importantly than a yes or no is that the answer be honest. It may be, "I can't work on the car today because I am overloaded with work. I will get on it first thing tomorrow, I promise." Any kind of honest answer is better than a yes to make the person feel good, followed by a failure to perform. I wish I could tell you how many times in the last twenty-four hours I said to myself that I won't be able to use that mechanic again. I will have to find someone else.

Once you get used to saying no, it becomes easy. You can learn how to say a pleasant no when someone is trying to sell you something. The more you practice, the easier it gets. Just learn to stop them early on in their presentation, make some nice comment about how much you appreciate their time in attempting to present their wares to you, and then say you won't be able to participate or buy at this time. You don't have to explain your reasons, because they are none of their business. Simply decline politely.

"I'll Do My Best"

If we would learn to say no, rather than string people along with "I'll try" or "I'll do my best", a lot of time would be saved. It makes you appear more dependable. Remember, if you say yes (or one of those other affirmatives), and then don't perform, you have tarnished your reputation for dependability. People will remember your decisive, dependable nature and be refreshed if you learn to give an honest no when you know that you will not be able to do the job right away. They will want to call you again, even though you can't perform for them now, because they know you will answer honestly. They know that if you say yes, you will do it.

The contractor I talked about earlier was not such a person. When you were finally able to talk to him after trying for days, you would know he meant no when he said yes. You could even ask him questions such as, "Are you sure you can do this?" or, "Are you sure you have the time to get this done?" Whatever the answer, you knew it would never get done. The answer meant nothing.

Priority Management

Most experts will tell you that time management is really priority management. Watch your goals and work the priorities, those activities that are high-leverage activities, those that put you closer to achieving the goals you set. Learn to work the priorities and say no to the activities that aren't getting you anywhere. As you have heard before, "never let the things that matter most be at the mercy of the things that matter least."

When you know how to say no, you may occasionally have to give up an opportunity that might have been fun, nice, or worthwhile. But your stress level will be much worse if you become someone who says yes to everything but only performs on some things.

In sales, such as real estate, it is very distressing to continue to work with and follow up on people who can't say no. How much time would be saved if they had said, "No, I don't want to buy it" the first time you showed it to them. Instead they say they haven't decided yet, even though they know they will never want that property. They just can't seem to be honest early on. Maybe they want to be nice and not disappoint the broker. But early disappointment is better than stringing someone out and costing him valuable time.

3. Meet Your Deadlines

Begin now to make it your priority to deliver when you say you will. Some people like to say they will deliver at a particular time just to get the job. I believe my mechanic friend said yes so I wouldn't go somewhere else. But that can backfire, because he may have lost my business permanently by not performing when he said he would. Those types can almost never deliver promptly and usually end up being labeled untrustworthy—flakes. When I was engaged in building and developing, I used to add a week or two to what the subcontractor would say it would take on certain jobs, and often this was pretty accurate. It's so bad in certain fields that a promise to finish at a certain time is almost a waste of breath. Once again, a guy can be the best in town at what he does, but if he can't finish when he says he will, people will think he is a flake.

Word of Mouth

Honesty is the best policy here. Tell them the truth up front. Tell them what you can do and when you can do it. Then do it. Usually, one of the greatest sources of business for a small firm is word of mouth. When someone calls one of your clients, you want them to be able to answer truthfully that you always complete the job when you say you will and that you always show up.

4. Punctuality

I have some friends and acquaintances that I can set my watch to based upon when they arrive. I call them twenty-minute-late people, or one-hour-late people. Some are on-time people. For example, when I invite twenty-minute-late people over for dinner, I tell them dinner will be served at 2:00 and tell my wife to have dinner ready at 2:20. The scheduling principle usually works out just right.

Then when they finally arrive, there are always those excuses. They may say their cheap watch stopped, or they just couldn't make it because of traffic. Whatever the excuse, the people listening know better. They would be better off just to tell the truth and apologize.

Punctuality Is a Value, and Valuable

In business, being late can label you and can cost you. This failing is particularly noticeable. It is a real slap in the face. Everyone has a schedule, and to show up late, or not at all, affects those schedules. It's just plain rude. Consider it a rule of etiquette if you want, but also consider it a business principle, a practice worth business and money.

Some people don't think this principle is important because every time they are late the people waiting for them always say something like "Oh, that's okay. Don't worry about it," or some similar comment. People won't be rude to you even though you were rude to them by being late. You will never be criticized, but you can be sure that they are irritated and unimpressed. No one will ever call you fat, either, but if you are, people notice.

Punctuality Is Honesty

When you tell someone you will be there at 7:30 and then don't show, it is almost like being dishonest. It's the same with being late, especially if you make a habit of it. Having a hard time with this concept, are you? I suggest that if you are a late person, you may be looking for counter-arguments to the idea that punctuality is honesty. But if you are an on-time person, you know the feeling. Being late creates distrust and the feeling that you have been let down.

Almost as bad as being labeled dishonest is being labeled unreliable. People who are consistently late run this risk. Therefore, they may not be considered executive material or may not be considered for advancement or some other recognition that they seek. Being late is a serious problem that can have many other, unintended consequences.

"Late people" should realize that they are being compared to "on-time" people. It may be an unconscious comparison, but nevertheless there are others around you who always show up on time and always have their work done on time. If you don't, it is very noticeable.

You Can Beat This Habit

Remember Murphy's Law: anything that can go wrong, will. Therefore, things usually take longer than you expect. You should budget more time than you think you will need to get where you are going. Plan on more time to get the project done. Time management experts suggest you add 25% to whatever length of time you feel you will need. They also say that in their surveys on business etiquette, 94% consider being on time correct and important.

Some people are consistently on time. To be late just a few minutes sets off a major guilt trip for them, and they become profusely apologetic. It's just awful to be late and almost never happens to them. For others, being late is just a way of life. They don't even realize that it's a problem. Apparently some people just don't comprehend the concept of the clock. They don't appear to realize how much their problem irritates others. It might be some ingrained hostility toward time itself. It may also be one of those unanswerable conundrums like those we have in politics and religion where we have to look to the hereafter for the answer. It's just a bad habit that can be overcome as soon as people are willing to recognize that they have the problem.

Punctuality in Other Countries

In Japan, if you are late for an appointment, you can expect to wait an equal amount of time before seeing the person you have set the appointment with. So far we haven't adopted the Eastern tradition, but we should learn the lesson here in the West. A word of comfort for you late people. In Central and South America, it is perfectly acceptable to be thirty minutes late. You may want to consider relocating! Better yet, consider how easy it may be to change your ways, break the habit, and start being on time.

Advice to Late People

If you think you might have a punctuality problem, listen up. Since late people don't like to admit they have a problem (who does?), let's assume you don't realize it. Consciously look at your watch when you arrive at appointments and see if you are there on time. Try recording how late you are at several appointments. If you recognize you have a late problem and are willing to admit it, consider the following.

Be Late to Anything but an Interview

Being regularly labeled a late person is hurting you. It shows that you are flaky and is an indication that you may be unreliable in other areas too. I have a friend who is a "head-hunting business consultant." He specializes in advising people how to properly interview and prepare to get new positions in business. He tells me that the number-one reason people don't get the job they interview for is that they are late to the interview.

Another friend of mine wanted to become a policeman, so he applied for a position in a nearby city. It was all he ever wanted to do in life.

However, because he was late for the interview, they made him wait two years to reapply. They said he must not have wanted the job bad enough. He eventually got the job, but needless to say, he went to the next interview on time!

Consider that it takes no more effort to be on time than consistently late. It is just a matter of habit and awareness. Don't go into a guilt trip and commit suicide if you are occasionally late. We are all late now and then. That is not the problem. Just realize that being habitually late gives you a bad reputation that you may not have recognized. Consider every appointment in your business worthy of your punctuality. There are certain things you just can't be late for. Make it your policy to be on time for everything, even the less important events.

Keep working on the problem until you have developed the habit of being on time. It will help your business and personal life alike. Remember, being late is the same as being a bad carpenter. You might be the best carpenter in town, but if you're late, you put your job or business in jeopardy.

Call Ahead

Finally, if you find yourself in a situation where you cannot avoid being late, call ahead, before you are late. Nine times out of ten, it will not matter to the client. But be late without calling, and it may very well matter. Being late without calling is like telling people their schedule is not as important as yours.

5. Follow Up

Want to go the second mile to show concern for your clients or customers? After you have performed your service or made a decent sale that day, call the client and see how everything is going. I have a dentist friend who does this each day. When he gets home at night, after having dinner and settling down, he calls the patients he has seen that day and asks how they are and if everything is all right. People just love him because they know he cares.

That kind of affirmative, voluntary, free act of extra-mile service can go a long way toward reversing other weaknesses and creating lasting good will. Remember, acts of this kind keep you in the 20% competence area where clients and customers aren't constantly out shopping to replace you.

In Summary

A reputation for being undependable may be seriously hurting you, even though you may not realize it. You might be a highly talented, capable performer in your field and still be considered flaky, simply because you don't do what you say you will do, or do it late, or don't call to keep your clients informed. You may even be carrying "lack of integrity" luggage without knowing it.

With word-of-mouth references being as important as they are in business today, don't allow yourself to be given a bad rap. Always call when you are going to be late and keep your clients informed. Learn to say no to unimportant assignments that will only hurt your schedule and distract you from the missions and goals that matter most. Always meet your deadlines or ask for extensions in a timely manner. Be on time for everything, especially when you promise you will be there at a certain time. If you want to go the second mile, follow up afterward when it is not required or expected.

You can be an excellent contractor but not be very busy because of a reputation for unreliability. But, conversely, by following the five points of dependability outlined in this chapter, you might be a very successful contractor, even if you aren't the best in town.

Chapter 6

Practice Three: Build Trust

The Practice of Developing Trust with Character and Integrity

A great checkbook can never make a great man. . . . Character is success, and there is no other.

Orison Swett Marden

The Character Ethic

The objective here is to convince the reader that the character ethic is not dead in business today. It is not a turn-of-the-century doctrine that has no meaning today. Character and honesty create trust in customers, and that means profits today, more than ever.

Take Advantage of the Little Opportunities

Character and honesty have taken a back seat to the bottom line in many businesses today. Businesses decide to sacrifice integrity for a quick boost in profits. They say it's not really wrong, it's just business.

When I first started my legal service business, I was trying to break into a large insurance company whose patronage would be a great boost to my little fledgling company. I had been introduced to one branch office and was trying to give excellent service in order to secure the other offices. I wanted to build my business, and getting them as a client would be a great asset.

Once they sent me a check for one of my invoices. The bill was for about seventy dollars. The check they sent was for eighty dollars, an obvious error for which I was eventually very grateful. At the time, I didn't think much about it. I was disappointed, because I needed the money, but I knew I was going to have to send back the check and ask for a new one. That would take a few weeks.

After a few weeks, the long-awaited check was sent to me, but it is what was sent with it that was the windfall. I received a corrected check for seventy dollars, along with a nice letter from the regional manager stating that my integrity was refreshing. They said it was nice to know there was still someone honest out there. I could have kept the extra ten dollars and no one would ever have known. Instead, without another thought, I had my secretary send it back for correction. Soon after, I visited that regional office manager. It was easy to convince him to introduce me to the other nine offices in his region. I visited them in time, and they all became good clients. And all this was because of one simple act of integrity.

That company became our best client. We eventually expanded our service to them, serving as many as thirty-five or forty of their offices. They liked our service and passed the word from office to office, because they could trust us. Twenty years later, I'm told they are still the best client of that little service company. Over two million dollars worth of business has been generated because of that ten dollars.

Don't Get Contaminated

Never let an act of dishonesty enter into your business practices. Once that happens, you will lose the trust of your client. To clients, it's like putting one drop of food coloring into a clear glass of water. It never looks the same again until it is all replaced with new, fresh water.

Trust develops after positive contacts and experiences. Once trust is there, it must be maintained for the business relationship to continue. Continued business relationships mean continued profits. Business can go on forever if there is trust. It can end quickly with one dishonest act. Honesty is one of the best sources of PR available. And it costs nothing. This is one of the most important, yet unrecognized, problems in business today. Many principled, honest people, active in their churches and communities, seem to have a different set of rules when it comes to business.

Trust Equals Profits

Unfortunately, the importance of this subject is not discussed much these days. There are ethics classes in some entrepreneurial programs, but frankly, most of it is lip service. Most of the discussion doesn't include the real worth of an honest attitude—its real dollar value. It doesn't include the damage done when a person is caught in an act of dishonesty. I'm talking about the purchase of millions of dollars of future business for ten dollars. You should hope for the opportunity to return a check that represents an overpayment, or for some other opportunity to demonstrate your business integrity.

Costly Attitude

The following is a true story about a friend of mine whom we'll call Glenn Sharpe. Before he retired, he was a contract negotiator for a large company, well known for its defense contracts with the government. His company, which we'll call Acme Defense Widgets, had produced an important software package for certain applications in the defense industry. They had also provided some proprietary electronic equipment to another large company, which we'll call Blowhard Defense Gadgets. Blowhard borrowed the software and used it to demonstrate the equipment, after agreeing not to use the software for profit. The agreement was put in writing and signed by both parties.

Glenn later found out that Blowhard Gadgets had made a bid to the federal government to produce and sell certain products, including the borrowed software package. Acme immediately confronted Blowhard and asked why they had violated the agreement and used the program. A meeting was set up at Blowhard's board room to settle the issue.

The meeting involved the CEOs from both companies, along with Glenn and other legal counsel. Blowhard first denied that they had broken the agreement. The written agreement was produced, showing the promise not to use the program. The bid document was then produced, identifying the specific document number and program that had been submitted to the Defense Department. The document implied that Blowhard had created the software program themselves, giving no credit to Acme, the real creators of the program.

After more denials, the Blowhard CEO finally admitted submitting the bid in violation of the agreement. He then asked whether the document they signed was really a legally binding document. Glenn answered that they were not sure, but ethics were certainly involved if nothing else. At the very least, a promise was broken.

The guilty CEO then said, "Mr. Sharpe, do you understand how the system works? Ethics are not involved. The only thing that matters is whether it is legal. And that does not matter unless you are caught. And being caught doesn't matter unless you are found guilty. And being found guilty doesn't matter unless the price of the fine you pay is more than what you got out of it in the first place."

He paused for a moment and then added, "Now, Mr. Sharpe, do you understand how the system works?"

Concluding that this was the way Blowhard regularly did business, Glenn Sharpe and Acme's CEO left the meeting bewildered. Blowhard Defense Gadgets is a large, well-known company that has served the public and the government for many years. If I were to mention their real name here, you would certainly recognize it. And this was their philosophy of business.

On the way to their car in the parking lot, Acme's CEO asked Glenn how much money he would need to establish a company of their own to provide the same products as Blowhard. Glenn said $35 million. The CEO said, "You have $17 million to get started now, and you'll have the remainder later, when you need it to complete the project." They established the company in that same city and successfully competed with Blowhard, depriving them of valuable contracts and capturing a significant market share of the valuable defense business there.

Later, the CEO of Blowhard was indicted by a federal grand jury for an unrelated incident. He was eventually acquitted for lack of evidence. Later, in a nationally broadcast news conference, he said, "See, I was never found guilty."

Light at the End of the Tunnel

Even though there is still abundant evidence of widespread lack of integrity in business, I believe there is light at the end of the character tunnel. In *The Seven Habits of Highly Effective People*, Stephen R.

Covey's basic theme is the return of the character ethic. He indicates that he was deeply immersed in a comprehensive study of the success literature published in the United States since 1776. He scanned hundreds of books, articles, and essays in the self-improvement, popular psychology, and self-help fields to discover what a free and democratic people considered to be the keys to successful living. What he found was extremely interesting to me.

In the first hundred and fifty years the literature concentrated on the fact that the foundation of success is what was called the character ethic. Integrity, humility, fidelity, temperance, courage, justice, patience, industry, simplicity, modesty, and the golden rule were the ingredients to enduring happiness and true success. Incorporating these principles in your life and into your basic character and nature were emphasized.

Sometime after World War I, the basic view of success shifted to what was called the personality ethic. This means that public image, attitudes and behaviors, skills and techniques such as a positive mental attitude, have become the emphasis for the last seventy years. These attitudes and behaviors are taught in today's literature and seminars as quick-fix, overnight ways to obtain success. It appeals to many people, because it is an easier, quicker way to reach goals or to get rich.

The fact is, quick-fix ways to get rich usually sound good but don't work. The lasting way to create wealth and success is to understand that you reap what you sow. Long years of showing honesty and integrity create long years of trust, which in turn create success in business. People tend to be drawn to those who show stability in character, rather than those who appear pumped up with positive mental attitude techniques of high-pressure salesmanship.

The Money Will Follow

There appears to be some movement in the business community toward the idea that giving of ourselves and providing quality and excellence in service should be the primary concern in business. We should focus on satisfaction in the way we provide the service and in providing the service itself, rather than in receiving the monetary payment for the service. When you cultivate an attitude of giving back, of contributing to society, clients and customers see the concern and depth of honest effort. The monetary benefits follow naturally.

It's Not Easy to Recover

When my firm was performing a secret shopping service for a large restaurant chain, we tried to hire people of integrity. You can imagine why. We were sending about twenty-five hundred people into restaurants and doughnut shops across the country. We never met face-to-face with most of them. They were interviewed and trained by phone and by mail. They had to be recommended by someone we knew or trusted. Notwithstanding our due diligence in seeking good people we could trust, we had our problems. One of our most trusted, pillar-of-the-community shoppers filled out his reports without going into the stores. He was caught easily by a complaining manager when he put something on his report about a waitress that wasn't working that day. That incident was hard for my shopping service firm to overcome. The mistrust that resulted set us back for some time.

I received a call from one of our shoppers who was upset because we asked for her Social Security number. We needed it so we could fill out her IRS Form 1099. She had been paid over six hundred dollars, and we were required to report it. This lady was upset, because if she made more than a certain amount of money she would lose her food stamps and welfare benefits. She didn't want us to send in the form so that her other local benefits would not be jeopardized. We sent the form anyway, because not sending it would have put my firm in danger of being penalized, or even guilty of fraud. I don't know whether she lost her benefits, but since I didn't like the idea of someone with those ethics being on our staff, she was released.

Thomas J. Peters and Robert H. Waterman, Jr., did some more encouraging work in their book *In Search of Excellence.* They studied large corporations to find out what made the good ones tick. As we should expect, the high standards of the good companies were conspicuously absent in most of the rest. While they don't mention much about integrity and honesty itself, it is refreshing to note that the good companies seem to be *value-driven*, concentrating on training their employees to provide quality, integrity, and good service to their customers.

Concern for the Other Guy

There is more to character than just honesty. Success literature has placed more and more emphasis recently on thinking win-win and being concerned about the welfare of the party you are dealing with. To sink the other guy for all he is worth will eventually backfire. Those who want lasting business relationships focus on trust and fairness, rather than on getting the quick profit. Who would get your repeat business? Wouldn't you go to the guy who had integrity, who treated you with kindness and understanding, who was patient and concerned with your position too?

The Fatal Mistake

People must begin to understand that honesty and integrity are business issues. They can yield enormous benefits, because honesty and integrity create trust, and trust creates business. This subject should be taught not only in Sunday School, but also in schools of management and entrepreneurship. Often I chuckle when I see someone flagrantly lie or attempt to cheat me to get my business. I just say to myself, "That poor guy. He just made his fatal mistake. He has not only lost this sale to me, but he has dealt with me for the last time."

A Prime Example

Businesses should be set up so that their policies promote honesty. Instead, however, they are often set up to encourage dishonesty. A good example of this is the auto repair business. The problem afflicts some auto repair shops, but it mainly involves the service departments of new car dealerships.

Placing auto mechanics on commission has never made any sense. It is hard to understand why a company would tempt its lowest-echelon employees to abuse such an important business asset as customer trust.

By putting the mechanics on commission, they are placing them in a position where they are tempted to oversell both parts and labor. Certainly there is pressure to produce from management. But these days, when people have to pay so much attention to where their dollars are going, it isn't the right time to try selling them parts and labor they don't need. Then again, when would the right time be? There never will be a time when it will be a good idea to establish a company policy that puts profits before trust. Companies should avoid the very appearance of violating a customer's trust.

Lo and behold, in mid-1992, right in the middle of writing this chapter, the national news media broke the story of how Sears had been accused of replacing parts and making repairs that were unnecessary. In California, the policing agency of the state had sent investigators into Sears' auto service stores and found fraud. This began a public discussion about the advisability of the practice of putting repair service advisors and mechanics on commission. Sears had implemented a commission system about three years earlier to improve sales.

Of course it would improve sales! When you give the low man on the totem pole the authority to increase his own income and, thus, the income of the company, what else would it do? Some people have never trusted dealer service departments for this very reason, and this may be a reason why they prefer to go to independent repair shops.

The California consumer protection officials said that at Sears there was a quota system that encouraged widespread fraud. They launched their investigation in 1990, because consumer complaints about Sears Auto Service had doubled after the commission system began. After this story broke, sales in their auto shops dropped fifteen percent in just eleven days.

Sears Finally Sees the Light

While it was nice to have this example to use here, it was even more impressive to see how Sears handled the problem in their 868 auto shops across the country. A few weeks later an article headline read, "Sears ends auto shop commissions." A consumer repair expert said it was probably the only thing Sears could do right now to restore their credibility. Their service advisors will now receive a salary that will approximate what they would have gotten in commissions.   Sears chairman Edward Brennan said, "When our integrity is on the line, we must do more than just react—we must overreact."

Sears should be applauded for returning to a system that establishes credibility and demonstrates integrity.   Many companies could learn a great lesson from them.   Create an atmosphere of trust, integrity, and credibility, especially if your line of business has a reputation for mistreating customers.

Lack of Confidence

I have never had confidence in the service departments of new car dealerships.   Maybe I have had bad luck, but I always feel like they take advantage of me.   They always seem to charge more than anywhere else, and new, full-price parts go on the car, whether they are needed or not.   That is the feeling I have always had.   I have always had better luck with independents.

The other day I took my van into the dealer for some warranty work.   That is usually the only reason I will go to the to the dealer.   While I was there I found it convenient to have some other work done too, rather than to take it to an independent later.   They gave me a preliminary estimate which didn't appear to be too bad, so I signed it and went out the door thinking they would call asking permission to do much more.   Usually the mechanic (who is typically on commission) will find more problems that require other new, expensive parts.

When I arrived to pick up the car, the service manager said they were still working on it because they were having trouble putting on a part.   It was taking much longer than they had estimated.   I didn't say anything, but I figured the labor charge would be higher than quoted.   When it was ready, I was surprised to find they hadn't charged me extra.   They charged me only for the original estimated labor time.   I was pleasantly surprised.

A Pleasant Surprise

Some weeks later I happened to meet the owner of the dealership. I immediately complimented him on the good service they had given me at his service department. I had always thought that if I got the chance to discuss the subject with a dealership owner, I would ask why they don't consider taking their mechanics off commission to create more trust with customers. I took the opportunity to ask the question. As I asked him the question, I thought to myself what a stupid question it was. I knew the answer. They made more money the commission way. But I finished the question anyway. His answer was as much of a surprise as the service at his dealership had been. He said his mechanics weren't on commission. I said I thought all dealerships had their mechanics on commission. He said maybe they are, but mine aren't.

I take my van there most of the time now. I trust them. If you operate a business that is similar to the auto repair business, where there is room for mistrust between the business and the customer, figure a way to bridge that gap, so the customer can trust you more than the next guy. You will find yourself with one of the busiest operations in town. If I owned an auto repair business, I would consider advertising the fact that my mechanics were not on commission.

The Idea Could Work in Any Business

This inform-the-public-up-front method of advertising trust and confidence would work in businesses that operate basically the same way as auto repair services. Many businesses do their work where the client can't watch them. Figure out a way to create a trust between the owner and the repair shop. Establish a comfort level and you may just see growth you didn't believe possible.

Auto repair is only one example. Recently my upstairs furnace made a loud noise and then immediately quit working. I called a heating and air conditioning company without knowing much about them. I had never used such a service in this town. The man looked briefly at the appliance and then said it would need a new motor. He told me what it would cost, and after I gulped, I told him to do what he had to do. He said he had a new motor in his truck and would do the job right then. I went back to my Sunday afternoon dinner.

When he was finished, I got out my checkbook and we sat down together. I expected to write a check for the amount previously discussed and authorized. He said that after he got inside the heat pump unit and could test the motor, a simple greasing and general service was all it needed. The cost was substantially less and I was pleasantly surprised. Needless to say, I hadn't had many experiences like this one before. I had found someone who could have easily charged me the full amount agreed to, but charged less because he did only what was needed. I now have a heating and air conditioning company I can trust and use in the future. My guess was that this guy was not on commission, and I was right.

These are the kind of steps you can take to create trust. Each little gesture will bring positive references from your clients, until you can't handle them all. Whatever your business, do what is necessary to set up systems that create trust. Such a system may cost a little in the short run, but you can expect net profits in the long run.

It Seems to Be the Norm

In our "caveat emptor" society, trust, honor, and loyalty have taken a back seat to profits, and have little meaning today. Business integrity is considered an oxymoron. Everyone checks up on everyone else before doing business with them. Credit checks, background checks, investigations, and lie detector tests are the norm. Surveys on ethics show that two out of three people believe there is nothing wrong with telling a lie. Even more shocking, only about one third truly believe that honesty is the best policy.

It May Be Difficult

I know some business people may struggle with this "do good, be honest" philosophy. And remember, I'm proposing that honesty actually translates into profits, since it creates trust. This may not be easy for some people. Profits have long been the measure of success in business.

Some people think that it is the only goal of business and that everything a business does should promote profits. Norman E. Bowie, director of the Center for the Study of Values at the University of Delaware said, "I contend that the more a business consciously seeks to obtain profits, the less likely they are to achieve them." He calls this the "profit-seeking paradox." He feels that there needs to be a "rethinking of the motives for making a business decision, the purpose of business, and the values that traditional business managers hold."

Here we are in the 1990s, and some people are still so motivated by profits that they sacrifice trust by implementing company procedures that send the public the wrong message. The character ethic shows signs of returning, and the sooner businesspeople change their motivation toward fair and honest treatment of people, the better off they will be. The goal of serving people well will provide the successful achievement of profit goals.

Ethics on the Rise

It is clear that the subject of ethics is just getting started in its return to the forefront of business policy. Honesty and ethics are receiving emphasis from every segment of our society, including politics and even religion. It's not easy to find much on the subject in the libraries. But it is beginning to show up in the literature, and Harvard, Stanford, Wharton, and other well-known universities are adding ethics classes. Companies are beginning to take a stand on ethics as well. They are creating company codes of ethics and requiring their employees to read and memorize them.

Honesty Can Be Measured in Dollars

While in recent history honesty and ethics have gained attention in all aspects of life and culture, the difference is that in business, honesty is measured in dollars. Honesty translates into profits. It is becoming an important business practice which is making its way into college courses. But honesty is also measured in losses. In *Good Ethics Good Business*, Jacqueline Dunckel states, "Unethical business practices have resulted in

$200 billion lost annually to white-collar crime while fines and penalties for law breaking add up to another $100 billion." We already know what can happen to a company's reputation when its unethical behavior becomes news.

Dunckel goes on to say, "As a small business person, you set up your business to make money. You risked not only your investment dollars, but your reputation to start your business. What you can learn from history, both recent and past, is this: if you want to be successful in business on a long-term basis, you must match your operational expertise with an ethical code of conduct practiced in every phase of your business. No exceptions! Why? Because history has proven that ethical businesses succeed in the long run and, to put it bluntly, because business ethics can be measured in dollars. Sooner or later, unethical businesses get caught."

A Lesson for All Businesses, Small and Large

People shouldn't think that this subject applies only to big corporations because more is written toward that group. It is even more important in small businesses, especially those businesses run by one or two people in a small community. Owners can be ruined if they slip up ethically in a small town. This is a lesson that should be learned by larger companies as well, and it appears that there is some progress here. Some of the larger department stores are getting pretty friendly when you walk in the door, and fairness and honesty seem to be part of their standard operating procedure.

A Code of Ethics

Companies are insisting that they will not tolerate unethical activities that benefit individuals or seemingly promote business profits for the firm. References to ethics are beginning to appear in company training and operating manuals. One said, "No one's bottom line is more important than the reputation of the Firm."

If you are involved in a larger operation and you don't already have a written code of ethics, push for one now. You need to catch up with the trend. It doesn't have to be so formal if you are a small company, but the tone for honesty and ethical behavior should be set by the owner so your business can grow and prosper. You must set the example as the owner and never deviate from the code of ethics.

Ethics programs don't need to be long, detailed handbooks about what to do and what not to do. Setting the tone and publicizing the mission of the company is more important. When people know your purpose for being in business, when they have goals to work toward, and when they know that ethics will be established and enforced, they quickly follow suit. Hiring good people and taking swift action against those who violate the standards are popular procedures in codes of ethics. Employees should be involved in the preparation of ethics codes and mission statements. This will make them more committed.

In Summary

Honesty and ethics used to take a back seat to profits. Now they finally seem to be getting the attention they deserve. Entrepreneurs need to learn early, during start-up, that it is no longer good "business" to get what you can for quick profits and then yell "caveat emptor" afterwards. Those kind of people don't endure. They just come and go.

Companies that endure promote codes of ethics and honesty in their procedures. Customers never forget little gestures of honesty such as returning a ten-dollar overpayment. They also never forget bad experiences, such as getting ripped off at the car repair shop.

It isn't enough just to obey the law. You can't measure your integrity by whether the prosecutor has the evidence to prove you guilty. Ethics and honesty go much deeper than that. Illegal and unethical companies usually get caught and eventually just fade away.

There is clear evidence that our country is moving toward promoting business through character. The big companies are moving that way. Little companies have always had to act that way to exist. People hurt themselves when they brag about how they cheated the IRS or how they got away with ·something unethical and made or saved some quick dollars. If you know that they are dishonest with others, you know you can't trust them to be honest with you. Even Al Capone wanted honest people to be around him—people he could trust.

We all need to get on the bandwagon. Rather than emphasizing profits, America is moving toward attitudes of win-win, empathy, character, honesty, and trust. Business leaders are learning that profits flow naturally from practices that develop trust. They are setting up codes of ethics and asking employees to memorize them. And they are moving from self-destructive company procedures to those that promote trust. America is finally learning that honesty promotes trust, and trust translates into dollars.

When you consider starting up a business of your own, begin with the long-term end in mind. Develop honest and ethical procedures now, and never deviate from them.

Chapter 7

Practice Four: Put Needs before Wants

The Practice of Using Prudence and Restraint in the Handling of Business and Personal Finances

'Tis easier to suppress the first Desire, than to satisfy all that follow it.

Benjamin Franklin

Good and Bad Times

Here in the early 1990s, the country is in tough times. Banks aren't lending commercially, international competition is stiff, and the federal government hasn't been able to help so far. It is clear that times change, whether or not you think they ever will. In good times, people think things will never change. In bad times, people continually look into the future for the light at the end of the tunnel. The light always appears, sooner or later, and it always eventually goes out again. Learn from this chapter that the businesses that survive, and the individual families that make it through rough economic times, are those who are always financially prepared for the worst.

Can Times Change?

I used to believe that the economic climate couldn't change so much. Like most people, I sometimes lived for the moment, both personally and in my business. In southern California, I found myself believing that there was no way you could lose in real estate. I was born in the early 1940s and thus did not experience the great depression days. Real estate had always gone up. Sure, there were some recessions through the years, but I thought that real estate would always go up. I couldn't understand why anyone would consider investing in the stock market when they could own real estate in southern California. With lots of real estate fully leveraged, a person could not help but eventually become a multimillionaire.

Many people lost money in the early 1980s, and even more in 1990, when the economy took a bad turn. In 1992, real estate sold for less in southern California then it had eighteen months earlier. Most people didn't think that could ever happen. Some commercial property sold for as little as fifty percent of its previous value. Can times change? Yes, they can.

While some people experienced losses, there were also many people who were prepared for the tough times. They had plenty of cash on hand to take advantage of times they always knew would come. Their businesses slowed, along with everyone else's, but it didn't faze them. They were able to ride it out.

Many businesses had to struggle to survive those tough times by cutting back operations and changing warehouse or office locations from high-rent to low-rent areas. Some businesses had to sell off assets to survive. Whatever steps they had to take to survive, most of them wished they had always practiced such prudence. It's interesting how you think when tough times hit you.

A Warning to Entrepreneurs

A warning to entrepreneurs starting new businesses: prudent financial management must take place from the very earliest stages of your business, not when times get bad and you have to change your ways to survive. The firms that implement prudence from the beginning, whether times are good or bad, seem to be the more successful companies. The flaky big spenders come and go with the economy. The idea is not only to endure, but to grow comfortably and reasonably through good and bad times.

The Answer

The answer to survival in tough times should be clear. It is to have enough cash on hand, or the ability to get it without borrowing, to survive the times when revenues are scarce. Hundreds of books have been written on how to do this, so I won't dwell on it here. My real purpose is to help you develop an attitude of prudence and maturity in financial management so that you can govern yourself properly.

Start-up Advice

Many people get nervous when they start hearing about some of the supposed requirements for starting up their own business, and some checklists that are distributed would scare off anyone. Checklists for business start-ups seem to include everything for every kind of business. Some steps are important for all businesses, some for just a few of them. Some steps are unimportant or even unnecessary. Many businesses start off on a shoestring, while some have all the funding they need. What is important is that you do what is needed for your particular business and not be frightened by well-meaning recommendations almost no business follows to the letter.

For example, most checklists include a requirement to have detailed plans. Those plans are supposed to include detailed strategies for funding. Where will all the money come from for everything you need? In good times, when financing is easy and funds are available, many businesses can justify being fully funded before start-up begins. It's as though businesses must open their doors the way a McDonald's would do it: fully funded, fully built out and furnished, and fully staffed with people waiting to serve you. McDonald's has to start that way (and they can afford it, by the way), but most businesses don't.

This chapter addresses the above issues while also discussing other common fallacies. As you read this chapter and other financially-oriented literature to learn about your own start-up situation, remember, every business is different. Search and take a close look at what you really need in your situation. What is required will depend on the nature and size of your business. Use the checklists and other start-up helps provided by the SBA (Small Business Administration), among others.

(See appendix C for our start-up checklist.) But by all means, don't get scared away and decide to go back to being an employee because you come across a start-up step that seems difficult or frightening. Few obstacles to start-up are completely insurmountable. Most are not as difficult as they seem at first glance. Some are much easier than you would ever believe. Don't give up on your goal to get started. Be persistent, and you will be surprised how easy things go. If you don't like what a checklist recommends, do it your own way. Just do it.

Common Fallacies

Some common fallacies about business start-ups are regularly heard from inexperienced entrepreneurs. They say you have to be fully funded and fully staffed before you can open the doors for business. For the proper image, they say, it is imperative that the officers of the company arrive at their fancy, impressive offices driving Mercedes-Benzes. Another common fallacy is that undercapitalization is the main reason for early business failure.

Let's get to the main point quickly and then explore in detail. Despite what you hear from bankers, business management PhD's who have never been out in the business world, or even the SBA, who supposedly wrote the book on business statistics, it is not necessary to be fully funded, fully staffed, or have the best of everything in order to be successful. Most businesses start with hardly any funds and no staff! No one really knows the main reason for early business failure. Business owners who go under don't publicize the real reasons. Who knows? But one thing is certain: there are popular, common fallacies that need to be addressed to put your mind at ease.

Let's take these fallacies individually.

Fallacy #1: It is imperative to be fully funded to start your business.

Do you have to have lots of cash to cover months of expenses and purchase all the necessary equipment and supplies? The answer is that it would be nice, but very few businesses do. In fact, many that start by bootstrapping eventually become worth billions.

Bootstrapping

My father started his law practice with enough money for a sign out in front of our rented house in Los Angeles and some business cards. He purchased a used typewriter and some basic business supplies. He was in business. Some years later he moved to an office, slowly furnishing it, and ultimately ending up with a very nice office with a decent law library and lots of clients.

I started my little legal service business by getting a business license, a post office box, a used copy machine, cards, and stationery. I'm not sure exactly what it all cost, but it was less than two thousand dollars, and I could have done it for less by leasing the machine. My business grew from one order in the first month, with me doing everything, to a fully-staffed, fully-equipped, busy investigative legal service business serving attorneys, insurance companies, and corporations.

Inc. magazine regularly publishes articles about bootstrapping (Sept. 1991 and Sept. 1992). They say that United Parcel Service, which started on a hundred-dollar investment, is now worth about $6 billion. Hewlett-Packard started with $538 and is now worth about $13.1 billion. Gillette started with twenty-five cents and is now worth $7.4 billion. H. J. Heinz Co. started with a nickel and is now worth about $10 billion.

There is no end to the stories that can be told about businesses getting started with almost nothing. They just all faked it at first. Sometimes nobody knows how strapped they are. Often the owner himself obtains the first order, makes the product or performs the service, delivers, collects, and follows up to see if the customer is happy—and does it all with no staff.

I had to run my business from an office, but since no one needed to see it, I did it from a bedroom in my house. Offices in the home are commonplace now, because business owners save rent, realize some great tax advantages, and have the convenience of working right in their home. Many people think it isn't professional to bring clients home. I think they would be surprised to learn that most clients don't care. In fact, they may be impressed.

In my work in commercial real estate I dealt with many start-up owners. I would work with them to find office, warehouse or retail space to conduct their business. The whole time I was showing them space they would be talking about their business and how great they were. I would find myself impressed, thinking they were really doing well. Then, at the signing of the lease, when it was time to ask for the first month's rent and the security deposit, I would be surprised by how often they would ask to pay the security deposit over several months rather than up front. Many would even ask if the first month's rent could be deferred. This was just another confirmation of my theory that you can't tell how people are doing from what they say. Many times they appear to be well funded but, when pressed, can't pay their first month's rent.

It was rare to have someone gladly hand me a check for the full rent and all the necessary up-front expenses when moving into a building to get started. That would only happen with the national chains or well-established businesses who were adding another location or simply moving. People never seem to have enough to get everything they want to start their business. They are bootstrapping and trying to avoid borrowing. And often there is nothing wrong with that.

Keep Your Overhead Down

Many start-up businesses begin with little overhead, with the owner wearing most or all of the company hats. Many companies don't have to display their offices or warehouse space, let alone their personal vehicles or residences. Of course, there are some items that need to be purchased, such as business cards, stationery, licenses, supplies, office machinery, and product inventory. But the rule of thumb for start-up should be: *obtain only what you need and keep your overhead down.* You can get what you *want* later when it is safe to do so.

Funding Sources

For those who decide they need to get external funding, to whatever extent, a discussion of funding sources and investors seems appropriate here. In the discussion that follows, remember, it is assumed that such funding is necessary. The decision, of course, has to rest with the start-up owner. But bear in mind that if the business can be started success-fully without seeking outside funds, most of the experts will tell you to avoid debt. It may interest you to know that there are companies that operate with no debt. To name just a couple that I am familiar with, consider NuSkin and WordPerfect. Try to do it on your own without giving up equity in your business to friends or relatives, even if you have to bootstrap a bit. If you must get funding, consider the following sources.

There are four basic sources of funding for start-up businesses. We will discuss them in order from the worst to the best.

Source #1: Banks

Banks are going to be the most difficult to obtain funds from. Banks are in the business of making money on their loans for the benefit of their stockholders and depositors. They are also highly regulated. Therefore, they are conservative by nature and will insist that the loan be a safe bet for them. They will want you to back the loan with either a good track record, security in property or other assets, or both. They take few risks, but they are a viable source of business loans and should be considered. Call your bank and ask them to send you their packet on business loans. You will learn a lot by reading it and applying for a loan. Other loan sources often require a couple of refused loan applica-tions from banks, so apply at several locations. You may be one of the few who qualify. But for most, some other source will have to be considered. Whatever happens, you can learn a lot from the material that most banks will mail to you just for asking.

Source #2: Equity Lenders

There are loan brokers who have funding sources with deep pockets and are just looking for business opportunities. They look for returns on their money that are better than usual, and they are willing to risk their investment for it. They prefer the higher-risk ventures, because they know that the higher the risk, the higher the potential return. The difference here is that they aren't looking to lend money at a good interest rate. They look for opportunities to invest. They want part of the action. They look for businesses that appear promising and have good management, and they negotiate a large equity (ownership) position. Often the share they take is above seventy-five percent. They almost always want a majority interest. These sources often will only invest in the larger firms, not the small, one-person, start-up business. For those of you who don't want partners or other controlling owners in your business, this is not your source.

To tap these sources, detailed and professionally prepared business plans need to be submitted. (For an example, see appendix A.) If the idea is good, if they are impressed with the overall business plan and its projections, and if they are convinced that the management team is qualified to make it work, they will consider investing. The broker who has the funding sources will screen the business plans, sending on their way those he knows will not fly. Make your business plan professional looking, with an impressive binding. Learn what to place in the plan so it isn't too long, and make sure that your first few pages explain the basics carefully. In most cases, that is all that will be read anyway. We will discuss business plans in more detail in chapter 9.

Source #3: Government Assistance Loans

The federally-funded Small Business Administration, along with other state and local sources, is available for many business start-up needs. Their loans often have security and qualification requirements also, but they are available where banks have already turned down the applicant. Your bank may still be involved in lending part of the money, while the agency lends or guarantees the rest. The interest rates are often better, and the amount you will need to put into the deal as a down payment is usually less. Your banker is aware of these programs and will give you the information you need to become informed about SBA loans. Contact your local city and county governments also. They often have economic development money to attract businesses to their community.

Source #4: Personal Source Loans

The best source of funds is also the easiest and most available to the majority of entrepreneurs. Qualification is usually relaxed, and interest rates are often the best. Repayment plans often have easy terms, and you don't usually have to worry about being sued or foreclosed on so rapidly. This source often requires no equity or security. The source I speak of is family, friends, and acquaintances who know you and trust you already.

Some people would argue that this source is not the best, because it ties the family to the business, and problems can contaminate relationships if the loan is not paid back. Also, if the lending family member or friend gets some ownership equity for giving the money for start-up, the relationship could deteriorate when things don't go just right. There is a discretionary decision here to be made by the owner. While some people are forced to choose this source out of necessity, it is still surprisingly common.

Factoring

Some firms survive by borrowing against inventory and accounts receivable. This practice, which is call factoring, is widely used and frequently makes sense. However, when things slow down, there can be trouble ahead for firms who must now pay back loans to the bank while sales have softened. This kind of practice should be used only when it is essential for survival, and then only while taking steps to avoid the practice in the future.

Most people don't realize how much they are really paying the banks for loans. They also don't realize how close they are to the edge as they walk the treacherous path of business finances. The bank's situation also changes. Banks can dry up in the middle of a project and cause real trouble for companies who rely on them.

What Can Happen

Late in 1989, I was in the middle of a nine-unit apartment development project in southern California. I had visited with my friendly banker who loved me when times were going well for everyone. I had shown I could borrow and pay back, and I had gotten the affirmative nod on this new project. I was told I would be granted the same loan terms as always: 75% of the appraised value of the property at 2% above the bank's prime interest rate. That was a fair deal at that time, and we agreed that I should proceed with the project and apply for construction funds when I was ready to start building. We were close enough in our individual estimates of the value of the project, and both of us felt that the appraisal would justify the loan.

I proceeded to purchase the lot, pay for plans, and get them submitted for a plan check at the city. I'm sure some of you see what's coming next in this scenario. The real estate market softened in California at about the same time. When it was time to move forward with the construction loan, the appraisal came in much lower than expected. The savings and loan crisis was just getting into full swing, and appraisers were pressured to be conservative for their banking clients. Also, the bank's lending policy changed from 75% of appraisal to 65%. The interest rate didn't need to change. The project had to be shelved for lack of funds.

The developers who kept on building and the companies who kept on operating despite tough times in California in the early 1990s were the ones who had sufficient resources that they didn't need to rely on the credit sources that had all but dried up.

Short-Term Versus Long-Term Debt

Many of you may have heard Ross Perot harp about the dangers of paying for long-term projects with short-term financing. While he was referring to the national debt problem, he was also speaking of an important financial principle. We can learn lessons from the problems of government and other businesses. Your business is a long-term project. You have begun with a long-term vision, and you want the business to exist for years and be able to weather any economic storms that may appear. So you should prefer long-term debt over the expensive short-term loans that drain valuable cash flow. If you are now in business and are strapped with high loan payments, consider refinancing to long-term debt, make a plan to pay it off as fast as you can, and proceed to do what the smart guys are doing—operate debt-free.

The Ideal Way

Once again, smart operators are operating debt-free. They may not start that way, but they get there as soon as they can. You can imagine why. Just consider your own personal financial situation. Do you like having to make payments on your credit cards, automobiles, furniture, and other accounts each month? I have never felt such a refreshing, comforting, stress-relieving feeling as when I paid off my cars, furniture, and other personal debt. Then I was entirely debt-free except for my house. To be out of debt is to be free. Companies can be in that same position. Look at all the companies that are going under, or selling off subsidiaries or other assets to relieve themselves of debt.

Leveraging

Society in general has become leverage-happy. We use leverage to buy virtually everything. The term OPM (Other People's Money) is popular, especially in investment circles. We buy homes, cars, and trips with credit. We purchase businesses, business equipment, and supplies, and we borrow against receivables and inventory with credit leverage. It has become the American way.

Sometimes it makes sense to borrow to get something done in a business. But the case for being close to operating debt-free is overwhelmingly convincing. The sacrifice is usually minimal in comparison to the potential trouble that tough times can bring. In some cases, debt may be well worth the risk. It may even be imperative. The owner must decide. But learn early that it is best to have little or no debt at all times, especially during tough times. Since no one seems to have the ability to predict bad times with any accuracy, it makes sense to stay out of debt from the beginning.

When times get tough, the companies who survive have little or no debt. If you have to tap a funding source, borrow only what you need, be careful how you spend it, and pay it back as soon as you can. Don't forget that often an alternative is to bootstrap a bit and to grow a little more slowly than you would like. You may be able to finance the growth with current cash flows.

Fallacy #2: You have to be fully staffed in all areas before you open your doors.

Do you have to be fully staffed with sales, marketing, accounting, office, and management personnel to get started in business? The answer is no. While all the above functions must be attended to, they can be done by the owner until the business can support hiring the help. Seldom do businesses get started fully staffed.

Fake It a Little

I talked about my father's law practice. When he started, he had no secretary. He typed his own letters with a used manual typewriter. At the lower left-hand corner of each letter the initials "JAJ:hs" would appear. The "JAJ" are his initials. The "hs" were the initials of the nonexistent secretary. I'll let you figure out for yourself what they stood for. Having figured it out for myself, I asked him why he didn't just put "bs" instead. He said that might be too obvious. (A hint: "h" is for "horse.")

Can you practice law without an office? My father did it. Another attorney would call and request an appointment at my father's office to discuss a case settlement. My father would say, "my secretary is away, so could we meet at your office instead?" They would always say yes and he would go there, parking his older car around the corner so no one would see it.

My father practiced law for about thirty-five years very successfully. He eventually got a nice office and a secretary. He had nice cars and a good life, and now he and my mother are enjoying their retirement debt-free. You don't have to be fully staffed at first for your business to endure successfully through the years.

I talked about my service business having no more funds than it needed. It also had no staff. My wife answered the phones at first, I did the field work, including the delivering, and we spent long hours trying to do everything. Later, when the business got going, we were able to relieve my pregnant wife of her duties by hiring a secretary. The business grew from no employees to eleven employees and about twenty-five hundred independent contractors helping across the country.

More *Inc.* magazine trivia. UPS was started in 1907 by a couple of teenagers delivering for local merchants. It wasn't until 1915 that they became motorized, using Model-T Fords. Hewlett-Packard started with a couple of engineers in 1938 using a kitchen oven to anneal the paint on their testing device. Henry Heinz began by selling out of his family garden at eight years old. He later formed H. J. Heinz Co.

Operate Lean on Personnel

When you start your business, use only the help you need, and be sure they are being kept fully busy and productive. Treat them well and make them part of your team. During the early months of a firm's life, the owner can fill in to see that things get done. Consider using independent contractors or even subcontracting out some work, or use help services. Your personnel are one of your biggest expenses. Be sure they are worth the expense.

Consider Outside Services

Janitorial, delivery, bookkeeping, and data processing services can usually be hired outside for less money. Take a close look at these costs and determine whether it would be best to use employees or hire such duties out. Each business is different, and the decision can only be made by the owner. Often, owners go to family members, knowing that the expense isn't any less, but the money stays home that way.

Some administrative duties can be subcontracted out these days. There are service businesses that provide administrative temporaries that can head up projects that need to be started. You may not need that most expensive employee full-time.

Fallacy #3: Fancy offices and expensive cars show success.

Are fancy offices and a new Mercedes necessary to show success? It is sad to see a new business owner immediately begin to spend that first influx of cash unwisely. The cash flow in a business can be a tempting thing to a recent wage-earner. Then you hear the car salesman tell you that you should get that Mercedes to show a better image. Some people can't resist the temptation, and they squander the newly acquired windfall on upgraded offices and furniture, and, yes, a fancy, new car.

Company Cars

Some companies use cars as a draw to get employees interested in working for them. Sometimes they are a necessity, but most often they are a luxury. If you need them, use them. If they are a perk for employees who are paid a little less, they may have to be used. But if you can pay employees to use their own vehicles, you may find yourself ahead of the game. If your accountant is not driving one of your company cars, he may be your best source to get advice. Leasing agents at car dealerships will tell you that everything is deductible. Don't listen. Get quality professional advice on this one. It is complicated.

I asked a wise friend once why he didn't purchase a fancy car for his business appearance. He was a business consultant who often took his clients to lunch. I knew what his answer was going to be, but I guess I just wanted to hear him say it. He said he wouldn't want his clients to see him is such a fancy car. He said he had to advise them and thought they would think him unwise to have spent that kind of money on something that will go down in value. People want to deal with advisors who are examples of prudence.

In case you haven't figured it out yet, leasing is the most expensive way to purchase a car and, in many cases, office and factory machinery. The interest rate is the highest, your mileage is limited, and your write-off is no better. Don't be fooled by what the leasing agent tells you. Almost all new car dealers have hired experienced leasing agents to get you interested in leasing. The cheapest way to purchase a car is to pay cash. The next cheapest is to finance it with a down payment. The most expensive way to get into a car is by leasing. Sure, it is tempting, because you can have that dream car without much down. Just make those large payments. And when you are finished making the payments you just give the car back. And you had better not have driven it much, or you will be fined.

Wait to buy that car until you can afford it. Sure, there are people who have all the money they need to buy the car but decide to lease because they have something better to do with that large sum of money. Those people know what they are doing and go into the deal with their eyes open. They have probably discussed the matter with their attorneys and accountants. Also, there are wage-earners who have absolutely nothing to put down, need cars for basic reasons, and can lease an inexpensive car. There are exceptions, but for the most part, to lease a car because you cannot afford to buy it is a mistake. A lot of money is wasted on cars simply because people want them. The best way to keep yourself in a decent car is to buy those cars that have been previously used by someone who turns them in prematurely. Low mileage, two- or three-year-old cars are heavily discounted. Give it some thought, but definitely see your accountant about leasing before you sign up.

This same reasoning applies to equipment and other necessities for your business. Which way do you go? Some companies are in growth modes and need to keep more cash on hand. Leasing can be helpful under certain circumstances. A good rule of thumb is to consider your needs in conjunction with good advice from your panel of experts, not your wants. What makes businesses endure and grow is concentrating on the quality of products and services and developing a good reputation for fair dealing. That should be the kind of image you want, not the false image of success that doesn't endure.

Operate Lean on Assets

When tough times hit, many companies begin to look closely at what they can sell that isn't vital to their survival. Maybe a smarter way would be to start lean and stay lean. If you are starting up, purchase only what you need, lease or rent if it makes sense, and operate lean until you can safely afford to extend yourself. You may be able to operate without extending yourself at all.

Save by Stepping down Office and Warehouse Facilities

When times got tough in the early 1980s, I moved my office back home where I started. A year or so after starting it I had wanted to get it out of the house. I didn't really need to. My business was the type that no one came to visit. We visited with clients in their offices. I wanted an outside office, but I didn't really need it. I could have existed operating out of my house. When times got tough, I moved it back into the home office. It meant substantial savings. When the business grew again, I had a real need to move out. I was careful only to get the space I needed, and I did not locate in the high-rent district. I've even heard of people who owned their office or warehouse but still moved their business into their home or garage to conserve cash. They rented out their space to others and created another revenue source that was helpful during lean times. Remember, do what you need to do, not what you want.

What Big Companies Are Doing These Days

We can learn some valuable lessons from what some larger corporations are doing in tough times. Many are consolidating facilities. I consulted with a Fortune 500 company that owned several different industrial service firms. They had been separately located for some time, and the word came down from corporate headquarters that wherever possible, the subsidiary companies should locate within the same facilities. The two companies now share the same warehouse and office facility. Tough times demand tough decisions.

The Grass Is Always Greener

I have always been interested in the subject of how people spend their money. I am a people-watcher when it comes to this subject. It has always been interesting me to see some rich people drive older, higher-mileage cars and live in modest homes. That has always impressed me. It didn't always impress me enough to motivate me to follow their example. On the other hand, I have observed people with no net worth buy (or in most cases lease) big, fancy, expensive cars and go into major debt to get that fancy dream house. My conclusion is that people spend according to their experience and comfort level with debt. Older people have lived through rough times and know the value of money more than younger people. Younger people are more willing to go into debt to achieve the richest lifestyle possible. As a people-watcher, I have concluded that you cannot tell what a person's net worth is by the car he drives, the house he lives in, or the clothes or the jewelry he wears. You especially cannot tell by what he says.

Business Image

A word about business image. Yes, your image means something. No businessperson would hire a management consultant who dressed like a bum and drove a rusty '49 Chevy. Cleanliness, neatness, organization, and moderation are more impressive than flashiness and excess. Going overboard on clothes and cars can backfire. My consultant friend bought a nice, decent, comfortable, middle-of-the-road car. People aren't fooled anymore. Anyone can lease a Mercedes with good credit. Success isn't your car; it's your reputation. Consultants are hired for their knowledge and ability to help, for what others have recommended about them, not for the clothes they wear or the car they drive. You can dress and drive for success by being moderate and saving all the money you would have wasted on a more expensive image.

Fallacy #4: The main reason for early business failure is undercapitalization.

The main reason businesses fail early is that they are undercapitalized. This is a very common statement that has only limited validity. Well of course they are undercapitalized! They spend all their capital on the wrong things, and then they don't have enough to survive. No one knows the real reasons businesses fail. The owners aren't required by law, under penalty of perjury, to state why they failed. No one likes to admit to having made mistakes. Owners will say that their failure was due to the economy or other external factors that were out of their control. No statistics are kept that accurately indicate the reasons. It is all speculation.

Many businesses that go under prematurely could have survived, had the owners practiced a little more patience, determination, and willpower. Although undercapitalization is cited as the major cause of business failure, there are other reasons being overlooked. Consider beginning with the end in mind rather than with so much emphasis on rapid growth in the beginning. Where are you going to be twelve years from now with this business? Will you be out of business or gliding along successfully? Being fully staffed and funded, with fancy cars and the nicest of everything (probably leased) is not necessary. Businesses endure and succeed when they consider what matters most. And it is not a purchased false image. They fail, not because they were undercapitalized, but because they used the available capital poorly.

Personal and Family Finances

If people regularly make a shambles out of their personal and family finances, relying heavily on debt and credit cards to buy almost everything, and regularly finding themselves in trouble when times get bad, they will almost inevitably carry that attitude and those practices into their business. They will also experience the same result—troubles. The businesses that operate with a budget and a well-established cash management plan seem to have less problems. Wouldn't a family be better off operating with a budget so they can know how much will be coming in and what is available to be spent?

From early childhood, most people are counseled to stay out of debt. This is one of those traits that most of us admire about older folks who have been through tough times, such as the great depression of the thirties. Many such people have millions in the bank but live modestly and still meticulously count their change at the store. If you know a banker, ask him about the terrible situations many people get themselves into because they never learned to get out of debt, stay out of debt, and live within their means.

As in business, money management and finances tremendously affect the success rates of marriages and families. The American Bar Association, with corroborating evidence from other sources, has concluded that somewhere around eighty percent of all divorces can be traced to quarrels and accusations over money. Professional counselors indicate that four out of five families are strapped with serious money problems.

It should be emphasized that these marital problems don't necessarily arise from lack of money itself, but from money mismanagement. The problems arise when the money management of a marriage is not a partnership with both members participating in the decision-making process.

Here are five suggestions for proper family financial management. Practice these procedures in your home and you will be teaching your family members and yourself the same attitudes of prudence and restraint that you should have while running a business.

The Five Practices of Prudent Family Finances: Lessons for Entrepreneurs

1. Make family money management a partnership. Whether your family has one money producer or two, the management of your family finances should be shared by both partners. Sometimes one spouse chooses to abdicate his or her responsibility of money management in the home. Or, conversely, one spouse often wants to control the money as a source of power and authority over the other. A cooperative attitude should be developed so that both members feel a part of the joint venture. This kind of attitude eliminates the opportunity for distrust to enter a relationship and sets up a path toward financial peace of mind. Such peace of mind probably has more to do with how money is mutually spent than how much is made.

2. Use a family budget. No business worth its salt could operate without a budget. It would be like committing financial suicide. Likewise, the family joint venture should have a budget where both partners know what is coming in and what will be going out in each spending category for every paycheck. Such a budget can be as simple as listing total anticipated income on one hand and a set of expense categories for outgo on the other. The expenses should total no more the income figure. Be sure to put in the hidden, easily-forgotten expenditures such as donations, estimated tax payments, and possibly savings.

Families that have a problem with one spouse overspending regularly will find a budget to be very helpful.

   3. Get out of debt and stay out of debt.   I can't tell you the relief my wife and I have felt in the last few years while ridding ourselves of our personal debt. It was such a good feeling to pay off those cars, furniture, and credit cards. With all the advertisements enticing people to buy and to use their credit cards, we have become a self-indulgent, keep-up-with-the-Joneses society. It took me about forty-five years to figure out that there is no glamour in the long and arduous task of paying the money back. The peace of mind that comes from operating with cash instead of credit is most worthwhile, believe me.
   Most people will have a mortgage on their homes because of the size of that expenditure. Many people will find it necessary to borrow to purchase a car. If so, it should be done with a large down payment and a short payoff period—preferably three years or less for automobiles. It is a good policy to rid yourself even of debt for your house and cars. When tough times hit, the people with little or no debt will more easily weather the storm. If you are riddled with debt and imprudent spending habits in your personal and family finances, you will see that problem carry over into your business.
   Some time ago, I was working with a small, single-owner company to find them a new location. They needed more space for their growing business. The owner wanted to buy a building or find a lot to build on. We looked at several locations but I was unable to satisfy his tastes and requirements for a good price and good terms. I finally determined that he was going to be too hard to please. Ultimately, it became clear that he was not capable of purchasing what he really wanted. He didn't have the money or the ability to obtain enough financing.
   I finally asked him what we should do next. What was his problem? Why were we looking at properties he couldn't possibly qualify to buy? He said he was building a new home, and he described the mansion being built for himself. Because of that, his cash situation was poor at the moment. We were unable to help him, and his expansion was necessarily placed on the back burner. Yes, decisions made by small businesspeople in their personal finances can seriously affect what happens with their businesses.

People need to learn self-discipline and self-restraint in their personal and business finances. Set personal policy about debt and spending and your life will be much more peaceful. In my client's case, his life might have been more profitable if he had used restraint in building his home. At least it is safe to say that he should have planned better for the necessary cash to operate both family and business.

Most people will agree that banks lend money only to people who don't need it. While that may not be entirely accurate, it has a grain of truth. Banks are very careful about whom they grant loans to. Their greatest concern is how those loans will be paid back. Learn from the bank policy and make this your personal policy. Borrow only when you absolutely feel it makes sense. Consider borrowing only for needs, not wants. Also, take out a loan only if it is easy to qualify for. If you have to beg for it and fudge on the application to be accepted, you should pass. Learn to "just say no" and be debt free.

Sure, there are times when owning your home outright is almost impossible. And some financial wizards would have you believe that owning your home with no debt would be an improper use of a great asset. Remember in the late 1970s, when the best advice was to use the equity in your home to make other investments so as to properly leverage your assets? While it may be true to a certain extent even today, don't listen. Do your own thinking on this very personal and important subject. If you are financially capable of paying off your home early, consider the decision to do so a wise one. While some people lose their homes in tough times because they were unable to make the monthly payments, those who own their homes outright don't ever have to worry about that. And if you are wondering about how wise the decision is to have no mortgage, don't forget the example of many companies, such as WordPerfect and NuSkin, who operate debt-free.

4. Maintain an adequate insurance program. Life, medical, auto, and homeowner's insurance programs for your family are musts! Overdoing insurance is self-defeating, but we have all heard some sad stories about how families are devastated because they lack the insurance to cover at least major catastrophes. Such losses can take years to recover from. If you have questions about what you really need, get advice from someone other than the agent you will eventually use to purchase the insurance. Insurance agents, estate planners, and stockbro-

kers make commissions on the amount they sell. Always get your advice from someone who will not be benefiting from the eventual purchases that they are advising you on. After you have decided what makes sense for you and your family, then go to the broker and make the purchase.

5. Maintain a savings account. Needless to say, maintaining an adequate savings account is an important part of proper family preparedness. Some advisors say to save ten percent of your income. Others say to keep six months' income available at all times. Probably better advice is to have a full year's worth of income safely in the bank for emergencies. Whatever amount you decide is best for you and your family, add something to it. In this case, the more the better.

In Summary

It takes maturity to face tough times. It takes even more maturity to know that tough times will come and to prepare for them. The time for prudent financial management in a business is while making plans for start-up. But it's never too late for existing businesses to plan for the next downturn by improving liquidity.

What's important is that business owners acquire a new attitude of prudence and maturity. I learned early in life that when you teach people correct principles, they can then govern themselves. "Give a man a fish and you feed him for a day; teach him how to fish and you feed him for a lifetime." What we should grasp here is that an attitude of prudence in financial management can make the difference in how long someone is in business. People without this attitude won't last. They come and go. Look around you at the people who have been in business for many years. They are not extravagant people. They practice prudence. It is one of their habits.

One book, or even several, couldn't cover all the various steps to curing all the cash management and cash flow problems of every business. But a leader with the right attitude can avoid them all. To start and run a small business can seem overwhelming from the outside looking in. Those who are involved in their own businesses are often surprised, looking back, at how easy it is when proper principles are followed.

Remember, you don't have to be fully funded, staffed, and organized like McDonald's to get started. Many new businesses fake it a bit and experience tremendous growth and success. Many start by totally faking everything without any funding. Some of them have truly experienced the American dream. Keep debt low, overhead down, and spirits up.

Chapter 8

Practice Five: Do It Well

The Practice of Delivering Good Quality and Total Customer Service

Excellent quality doesn't happen by accident. You have to plan for it.

Fran Tarkenton

Quality Service

Of the Seven Practices of Enduring Businesses, providing quality service may afford the entrepreneur the greatest opportunity to cash in on an American business weakness. So few businesses are providing quality service and building quality products right now that demand for quality from the public leaves open the door of opportunity. There are great opportunities in the service industry especially, where the majority of new business appears to be going in the 1990s.

Whether you are just starting up or are already in business for yourself, commit to providing your clients with what they bargained for and more. When I was an insurance adjuster just out of college, my experience in using legal service businesses was that they were slow and made many mistakes. When adjusters ordered medical records, they always needed them delivered faster than any of the firms were doing it for them at the time. Whenever I had to evaluate the claim of an accident victim, I would order the medical records. Usually I had to wait weeks to get them, only to find out that they didn't include everything or that they were impossible to read. Occasionally they were the wrong records altogether. Investigations that were ordered from outside firms seemed to take forever and often had to be done over for lack of detail and quality.

It wasn't difficult for me to decide what business I was going to start after my experience with using these legal service firms. As I mentioned in an earlier chapter, I leaned back in my chair, put my feet up on my desk, turned to my fellow adjusters in the room, and announced that I was going to go into business, but I didn't know what kind. This was in 1972, before the importance of quality service began to receive wide attention it enjoys today. But the decision was easy. I had already picked up some valuable experience dealing with service firms in my young career, so I knew there was a need for better performance in that area. I knew it would only take common sense to figure the business out. I didn't have many resources to get started, but I knew I was going to start something up that year. It was easy to decide to get into the service industry.

The Field Is Ready to Harvest

Today, in 1993, the field is still ready to harvest. I looked at the service companies I was using back in 1972 and decided that I could easily beat their delivery time and service quality. It couldn't be that difficult to keep in touch with the clients and keep them happy. The same opportunities exist today. There is still a need for reliable organizations that deliver quality products and quality service in every field. While most business leaders are apparently napping, you can get in on the service quality revolution that started just after World War II and continues today—and will continue until we get it right!

If you are thinking about quitting your job and going into business for yourself, don't deceive yourself for a minute that you will be able to fool the public with low-quality products or bad service. There are very few businesses that survive with such policies. The public is not stupid and will not endure poor quality any longer. I stand by my 80/20 Principle of Business on this subject. So few businesses are really concentrating on quality, especially in their service to the public. It just isn't that difficult to participate and get your share of the market.

Proper Company Policy

The commitment to quality must be solidly embedded in the written and unwritten policies and mission statements of your company. All employees, from the top level of management to the entry-level workers, must be committed to passing these practices on to those you serve.

I recently met a man in the waiting room of a tire and auto repair service agency. I had had good experiences with this company in the past. We were both waiting for our cars to be worked on. I was having tires put on, and he was in for a lube and oil service. He had called in by telephone to ask if they could change his oil right away. He had told them that he didn't have much time and couldn't wait, since he was leaving on a trip later that day. He was told that they weren't very busy that morning and that he could come in right away and get it done. He was at the store within fifteen minutes. He reminded them that he had called ahead and once again asked if he could be taken immediately. He was assured his car would be put right in and he proceeded to the waiting room. About thirty minutes later I appeared in the waiting room after ordering four new tires for my car.

After a few minutes, we began to talk. The discussion quickly led to service by companies such as this one. This was not only because of my interest in the subject, but also because he had now been sitting in the waiting room for about forty-five minutes, while his car was still plainly visible in the parking lot where he had parked it when he arrived. It had not been put right in as he was promised. What was worse, mine was put in quickly and was being worked on while his was still parked in the same spot.

We tried to analyze why my car and others would have been put in front of his. We were both fairly seasoned businesspeople, and we came up with some possible excuses. He was a patient man and didn't go to the counter to ask about it. He just sat watching his parked car. He had more patience than I would have shown.

My analysis was that it was possible that they put more profitable jobs in front of twenty-two-dollar lube and oil change jobs. That would be a mistake, since good service on a lube job might lead to new tire sales later. Their system for controlling job flow may have been flawed. Who really knows? The shop made a big mistake in failing to notify him that his job was being delayed. But worse still was not telling him when he came in that they would no longer be able to keep the promise they had made over the phone. Many problems can be avoided simply by keeping customers informed about the status of their jobs. Whatever the reason, my friend was certainly turned off and was not likely to return to that establishment for future business. Even though my previous experience with them was positive, this was a negative withdrawal from my bank account of good will that the company should not have made.

Doing Whatever You Have To

I mentioned earlier that there is a department store in our area that stands out above all others in quality of merchandise and service. It stands out in many other areas of the country also. In an interview with one of their salespeople, I was told that they are so concerned about their reputation that they go to great lengths to protect it. They want people to have a good experience in their store no matter what.

The employee told me that they were instructed to take back any item that was being returned, even if they knew it hadn't been purchased there. They were instructed to take the item back, even if they knew the person had just picked it up off one of their own racks and walked it over to the counter for returns. I asked why they would go to that extreme. She said that they were told they never wanted any other customer to witness anyone being argued with or being treated negatively. Even if they knew the item had just been stolen? That's right. She told me of an experience where the person was later arrested out in the parking lot for theft, but no one noticed any problem in the store. Total quality merchandise and totally positive service are the only experiences they allow in their stores. Salespeople wait in line for the opportunity to work there because they are paid more and treated well. Customers are willing to wait in line, too, because of the way the salespeople are trained to treat them. Yes, you pay for the service and fair policies there. But it's worth it.

Affordable Level of Quality

Everyone likes good service and fine quality merchandise. Very few people feel differently. Some people, however, are not able to pay for it. There is a clear need for someone to provide a level of service and quality commensurate with a bargain price. That is okay. The rule is not difficult here. Set your prices to create a fair profit, or you will not make it. Provide the best possible service and the highest quality product you can and still make a fair profit. Concentrate on the service and quality first, set the price to compensate for the expense of creating the product and service, and worry about the profits next. Companies are learning that they need to get their minds off the bottom-line profits and concentrate on the people and the service they are providing to them. Remarkably, profits flow as a result. Customers somehow figure you out when you concentrate too heavily on profits at their expense. They like to think you are trying to legitimately serve them and give them more than they bargained for.

I was listening to a radio talk show the other day where the interviewer was talking to a psychologist with a therapy practice. The interviewer asked why he chose to get into the practice of psychology. He said he wanted to help people and fill a needed gap. I have heard the same thing in interviews with CEOs of large corporations. They always cite some altruistic or philanthropic motivation for being in the business. I sometimes say aloud when I'm in my car, "Oh, sure! You're in it for the money and you know it." We all know they have to protect the investment of their stockholders and make a profit. If they didn't, they would not be in business long. Business leaders know this. The smart ones have figured out, however, that concentrating on profits to the exclusion of other important practices, such as quality service, leads them down the wrong path.

What Is Quality Service?

If you were to put the question "What is quality service?" to fifty different people, you would get fifty different answers. Service is subjective and personal. It is difficult to define. All of the answers could be valid, because each person can have a different, personal definition of what pleases that person. The same service by the same salesperson at the same store may result in different reactions from different customers.

In the law, you take the plaintiff as you receive him. This means, for example, that if you accidentally injure someone who has preexisting injuries, you may be liable to provide compensation for the previous condition if it is aggravated by your negligence. Each plaintiff is different and you take them the way they are.

It is the same with service to customers in your store, and that is the reason it is sometimes difficult. Each person may perceive the same service quality differently. I used to take pride in my client retention rate. I thought at one time I had never lost and would never lose a client. But I found out later that no matter how hard you try, you will lose a few. There are other reasons people choose to go somewhere else (such as their relatives just got into that business), but by and large, when you use your common sense in choosing how you perform your service, people will be attracted to your business. Remember, it is my guess that less than 20% of the businesses in any given field are doing really well in performing their services. Unless people have a relative in the same business as you, they will be your customer.

What Is a Quality Product?

The definition of a quality product is also in the eye of the beholder. It doesn't seem to matter what the producer and his employees think about it. What customers expect is the all-important barometer. Furthermore, customers' expectations can be based either on logic or emotion.

Ask a residential real estate agent sometime, or a car salesman, or anyone who sells to the public. They will tell you they may have the best, most reliable product on the market today, but if it doesn't feel right to the customers, they won't buy it.

Everyone is different. Have you ever heard someone extolling the virtues of a political candidate that you thought was a complete jerk? People are a product of many different influences in their lives. People come from different backgrounds and are as different in their politics or religions as they are with what satisfies their service needs. Everyone has different needs and wants, and to make it even more difficult, those needs and wants are constantly changing.

Pay Attention to What Matters Most

There is little room for disagreement on how to solve the problems of differing perceptions of quality. Everybody seems to agree that it is important to know your customers and clients and come to understand their expectations. It is only when their expectations are understood that they can be served accordingly.

This is where most organizations fall short in the area of quality competitiveness. They are thinking too much about the bottom-line profits and not enough about what is satisfying the customer. They don't take the time to meet the customers. They don't listen and talk with them and observe them actually using and appreciating their product or service. They don't pay attention to the customers. Owners should spend much of their time this way and be sure that their key people do the same.

Owners, as well as the people that make the key decisions, spend too much time running things, putting out the daily fires, and managing by crisis. While concentrating on day-to-day operations and month-end profits, they ignore input and observations from their customers. Customer input should influence new services and new products you are developing. They will also give you ideas that you can implement to improve what you are now doing. How else will you know exactly what they want?

Also, a good deal of your planning time needs to be devoted to analyzing the products and services you provide and making plans to improve. Some business owners take all their key people to a retreat to get them away from their day-to-day crises and devote full time to improvement planning and analysis.

Economics versus Customer Satisfaction

Customer satisfaction is just one of the measures of quality that owners and managers need to consider. Manufacturers also need to consider, among other things, whether the product conforms to planned specifications and whether it is maintainable. But the most difficult question has to do with the economics of providing quality.

There are many examples of companies that have overdone product quality, only to give up a major market share to another firm that provided a more general-purpose product that suited itself better to what the public demanded.

This problem is usually caused by the research and development engineers overdoing a product plan in an effort to make it perfect. Owners can't forget that quality costs money and that such expenditures have to tie back to a source of revenue to cover them. Expenditures cannot be indulged in disproportionately in planning for quality. There must be controls by decision makers who are responsible for profits and return on investment.

Somewhere in between quality that is too expensive and quality that satisfies the customer is where firms need to be. The answer is individual and difficult. Maintaining quality in manufacturing cheap plastic toys is a different task than when you are making precision surgical tools. There appear to be no hard and fast guidelines that every firm can follow. Suffice it to say here that each firm needs to establish its own policies and guidelines and decide how much it can afford to devote to quality assurance. Then, of course, it will be necessary to follow up to see that the customer agrees.

Attention to Quality Service

When I started my legal service company in Southern California serving attorneys and insurance companies, I knew that my principal business, my stock-in-trade, was service. I was handing my customers some records or reports nicely packaged in the form of a product, but it was clearly a service business and I always considered it such. Almost anyone could go copy records, and many people could be good private investigators. The actual work was not difficult to do well. It was timely delivery of a completed job that was important. Getting it fast and complete was essential to attorneys. Each delivery was important to me. If I had to go to extra expense to get it there by the time they wanted it, I was willing to do it. I couldn't let them down. Each little mistake might have meant losing that client—and all the clients he might refer to me later.

Often I would worry about an order that I thought was late or that had taken a long time to complete because of other people or circumstances that were out of my control. If I didn't get a delivery to a customer by the date that was specified on the order form, I would be sweating out the moment I delivered it, wondering if I was going to get a major chewing-out. Or I would worry about getting the dreaded complaint phone call before I could deliver the order. Often, however, the result would be that the customer wasn't irritated at all. He would say, "Oh, that's okay. I got a new court date and I have another sixty days to get ready. Don't worry about it."

I always felt better after a response like that, but I knew I couldn't let up. That is one of the problems with many service businesses. You must never let up or take advantage of the guy who is easy to work with. You must continue to put out whatever is necessary in money, time, and effort to serve that client better. You never know when another service like yours is knocking at his door. If he has no reason to let you go, you will certainly be in a better and stronger position. Profits gained from spending a little less to satisfy customers can't compare to profits lost from customers defecting to competitors.

What Big Companies Do

There are, of course, different procedures that larger corporations need to follow. Small businesses run by one or two people often find themselves in situations that large corporations don't have to deal with. This book is primarily directed toward small businesses, especially the start-up entrepreneurs. Start-up companies that master the seven practices described in this book from the beginning will experience a much easier growth path in the future. It takes a lot of effort to correct long-standing problems and policies in large corporations. The principles and practices, however, obviously apply to all companies, no matter what size. In fact, many good lessons can be learned from large corporations and their highly trained leaders.

Large, competitive companies with a reputation for quality spend enormous amounts of money to improve that quality. They bend over backwards and go more than the extra mile to keep quality at a high level. They are well aware of what is going on in the business world today. It is a war over quality. Some companies are winning market share away from others because they have found out what customers want, and they give it to them.

Federal Express, for example, is constantly studying and analyzing their procedures. When times get tough or bad luck hits them, they just continue to invest in quality improvement to combat the problems. For example, several years ago a cold wave struck Memphis, which is their national hub. As a result, pipes burst and damaged their computers. In response, they simply directed more effort toward making up the possible lost profits. When they started to lose a segment of the market because someone else had been performing a little better, they simply stepped up their costly quality-improvement programs.

Many large companies are instigating zero-defect quality-improvement philosophies and programs, sinking large amounts of labor and capital into providing better service. They have learned that sixty percent of the gross national product is service-related business. Two-thirds of all employment is accounted for in the service industry. There is plenty of business out there for everyone, but big firms like to dominate market share. They do it with large expenditures to measure the quality of service and to develop programs to improve it.

Small companies, take heed. Large corporations are paying close attention to quality, especially in the growing service-related industries. There is a revolution going on in the business community, and the quality of products and services will be improved as a result. If it is so important to them that their researchers and market investigators, like their counterparts in academia, are concentrating their studies on the subject, entrepreneurs should consider it important enough to include in their very earliest business plans.

Pricing

Services are less price-sensitive than products. While there is competition between service companies, generally higher prices can be charged for services. I found in my business of serving attorneys, insurance companies, and corporations, that people were willing to pay for good service. If my prices were in the ballpark, meaning not too excessive, my clients were happy as long as the service was good. There were always comments from clients and prospective customers about prices, but it was mostly lip service. Everyone seeks the lowest prices possible, but when it gets right down to it, the service really means more to them, especially if the people ordering the services are not the ones paying the bill.

For example, attorneys order outside services even on their contingency fee cases, and the client ends up paying the bill for them. Such services as private investigations often come out of the client's portion of the settlement or court award. Insurance company adjusters order investigations of accident cases, but while they enjoy the service, their company pays the bill. Corporations do the same thing. The large restaurant chain was sure willing to put out the money when it came to having my firm check their stores for quality of service. Companies do watch what their employees are ordering, constantly trying to keep their outside service expenses to a minimum, but by and large the employees have a free hand to order the service that will best serve them. And when they want fast service, they will order it from the company that can deliver it the fastest.

Every company must make profits in order to survive. Yours will be no different. Consider charging what you need to be competitive, but charge also what is needed to maintain the level of quality that will help your company endure.

America's Record

Unfortunately, the literature of the trade is showing that American service companies, for the most part, are not doing very well in providing their services to their customers. Most companies still struggle with the idea of spending money to achieve quality results. They haven't set proper quality goals and show few plans to improve. It just isn't a priority with many firms.

Learn another lesson from the large service provider Federal Express. During that heavy snow storm in Memphis in 1988, many of their flights were delayed, and therefore the delivery of many of their packages was late. They bought a fleet of snow plows so it wouldn't happen again. They are all painted with company colors, neatly parked and ready to go when they are needed for the next large storm. I'm told that the fleet of snowplows is used about one night every two years. Federal Express says that they have them in case they are needed, because a storm like the one in 1988 can cause delays, and delays are unacceptable.

It is that kind of attitude that promises good results in the service arena for Federal Express and those who think like them. Companies that don't begin to develop this kind of thinking well certainly not endure.

Take Advantage

Start-up entrepreneurs that are going to have service as their stock-in-trade need to take advantage of the fact that there are a large number of poor service companies operating everywhere. Remember, most people that use services like yours are dissatisfied with their current level of service and looking for another source. I believe the level of dissatisfaction is around eighty percent. It may be even higher. That's a lot of business just waiting to be picked up by someone willing to put forth the effort to do well. It's called an opportunity. My son is planning to start a small, service-oriented company in our area while he goes to college. I told him to get his business plan together and get started. It doesn't make any difference how many others in the area are doing it. There is plenty of business, and the people need you. Take advantage of the need. Take advantage of the percentage of companies that are not performing well for the public. Go out and compete. It's the American way. You'll be cashing in for yourself and at the same time adding a welcome quality company to the world of business. Just do it!

Many business leaders are noting a transition in the basis of our economy from manufacturing to service. It's a trend we cannot ignore. This fact was mentioned often in the 1992 presidential election campaigns. It has also been said that the 1990s is the decade of the entrepreneur. That is why this information for entrepreneurs is so important and timely. One of my purposes in writing this book is to teach these ideas of quality and fair dealing to start-up entrepreneurs so that they can experience success in the business world. Service entrepreneurs have a special responsibility to customers, employees, and stockholders to provide leadership in this area. Despite the challenges in achieving and maintaining quality in service, leaders must begin to seriously address quality if they are to remain successful.

There isn't any question that American business is developing an awareness of the importance of quality service. You see more quality service advertising all the time. They are beginning to zero in on it and are recognizing that the American people are fed up with poor service.

My firm was hired by a large restaurant chain to perform a secret shopping program. We visited each of their restaurants in North America twice a month and sent the reports to top management. In all, they had us visiting over forty-five hundred locations each month around the country to check the quality of their service policies. That fact alone was eye-opening to me. It was interesting to be in on top management meetings and hear the talk about what needed to be done to improve their quality service image across the world.

We met with their top operations people, often including the CEO. I saw amazing results in the computerized printouts following the input of our shoppers' reports. They showed greatly improved service times by waitresses as well as improvement in other quality areas. These kinds of programs being implemented by the larger companies show how much they are willing to spend on efforts to regain the service reputations they may have lost in the past. It also shows that maintaining service quality is not easy. It comes hard, with much effort and expense.

How Quality Service Is Initiated

What is different about a service, as compared to a product, is that service is personal. It is performed by people. The contact is with people. The difficulty is that service is harder to control since the front-line people produce the product (service), often when they are alone. Owners and managers must inspire and motivate them, but the real control rests with the trusted employee.

That restaurant chain wanted to check their service. Most large chain companies, and many smaller companies with a single location, do the same checking secretly. How can three regional operations vice presidents, or even the regional managers of a twenty-five-hundred-unit company really know how people are feeling about their service in each location? So they hire companies such as mine to secretly check them. They usually use regular, everyday, general-public type individuals that can tell them what it is really like visiting their locations. Usually the employees are notified that secret shoppers will be entering their stores, but they aren't told when or who. In the case of my client, the bonuses for each level of management were based in part on the report response.

Others leave small anonymous-response cards on the restaurant tables or near the cash registers. They hope that the public will comment honestly, and the comments are forwarded to the home office for review. Some owners sit down the street with binoculars watching their employees operate their companies.

Whatever owners and managers do, quality service doesn't just happen by accident, as Fran Tarkenton states. It must originate at the top. It begins with a desire to accomplish it and ends with a plan that is thoroughly implemented. Inspiration and motivation must come from above, or service will fade. Employees will, of course, adjust their service to customers in a positive way, not only after being inspired and motivated verbally, but as we discussed in chapter 4, when they are happy in their jobs, and when employers are treating them well. Employees' success with customers is directly related to the owner's success with employees.

Case in Point

In Ross Perot's campaign, he made the point that we the people own the government. They are *our* employees. We own them and pay them for their service to us. Yet what they give back to us, government service, is often called an oxymoron, a contradiction in terms. Shouldn't we get good service from our "employee" civil servants? Maybe there is a lesson we can learn here that could be applied to business.

The term "civil servant" makes a good oxymoron itself. Why do we always feel our civil servants are more concerned with their job security than our needs? One reason may be that total quality service programs and training cost too much money and take too much effort to get going. Then there would have to be expensive follow-up programs to measure and refine progress. Could it be that by not implementing expensive quality service programs, the government is saving us, the taxpayers, money? As in some of the giant companies that depend on success in the service area for their survival, where money and effort are expended, results follow. Where the incentive is survival, there is almost no alternative. Service must be a priority.

When the government example is turned around, we note that people have to go to the government for necessary services. It isn't a profit-making enterprise. If it was, as Mr. Perot has observed, it would be broke. Profit-making companies should learn from the government's example that to get people to want to use you takes more effort and expense than if they have to use you. But the effort and expense must be expended.

Whether the government example is a valid comparison must be left up to each of us to decide. In the government, like any company, the decision has to be made about how much of the available resources will be spent on service training and service program implementation. If we let the government spend more on a service improvement program and ask them to promote better treatment of our civil servants, we might see improved treatment of the government's customers.

Service Industry Profits Are Up

It is clear that less than twenty percent of all companies are truly committed to improvement of service by working toward the zero-defect level. Those companies have figured out that service companies overall are showing increased profits, where manufacturing companies are showing a decline. They have rewritten their mission statements and are pursuing service excellence. After counseling entrepreneurs, speaking to them in seminars, and working with them, it is clear to me that service businesses need drastic improvement. They need to start considering who they serve and who gives them their revenues. They must begin planning the programs to enhance the way they serve. With service profits up, there is every indication that owning a small service business may be the wave of the future.

Service Is Everybody's Business

Don't think that because you are in manufacturing and your business is product-oriented that you are exempt from principles of service. *Every business is a service business.* Some have to concentrate on service to a greater or lesser extent for various reasons. But all businesses provide service. When a product is marketed, there are plenty of contacts with the public in presenting the product and backing it up with service and warranties. Maybe your business is wholesale and your service is to your retailers. Business in the 1990s is service, no matter what the subject matter, and it is becoming more and more important as people are demanding better service from all firms that supply goods and services to the public.

An Attitude

We know that service can be a complicated procedure. It can be expensive and has proven to be difficult for larger firms who are fighting in a global economy to get a major market share. But my purpose here is to convince the reader that quality service is an attitude or philosophy that has its physical equivalent in the form of methods and results.

Those who intend to start a new business should enter knowing the importance of quality service and desiring to develop an attitude of service within their company personnel from the very beginning. Without this attitude, the company will not make a major impact in the market. It may only exist with a certain small, natural market share, and it may even fold.

If you have a very small business, the task will not be as difficult. To implant an attitude of customer service takes leadership. Much is talked about in the business literature about creating a "culture" in companies. Getting people to work together happily to serve the all-important customer is what leaders must accomplish. Whether it's giving freedom to employees to generate better results, or just paying them more to keep them happy, you must get your people working together as they would on a rowing team—moving straight forward as planned, each putting forth the best effort possible to succeed together in taking care of the customer.

How to Do It

This is not a detailed how-to book. My aim is to instill attitudes by teaching principles that successful companies now use. I have suggested reading the best books devoted to the details of how to develop a particular practice in your own situation or business. Each different business will require different quality-implementation programs. They are all individual. Here are some comments.

My restaurant chain client chose to implement a secret shopping program with bonuses linked to the results of the reports made from visits to their restaurants.

Hal F. Rosenbluth and Diane McFerrin Peters, in their book *The Customer Comes Second*, discuss an incentive program which they figured cost less to deliver than the usual expensive employee incentive programs. It gave points for accuracy, professionalism, and productivity. They didn't expect productivity would increase until the first two criteria were well established. The incentives were to be paid based on the points. Reports and feedback went immediately back to the worker so they could correct mistakes on the spot when they were fresh on their minds. The lessons could be used right then, on the next assignment, and the employee's points could immediately improve, and so could the service they provided.

Rosenbluth figured this program would cost them money but hoped to increase quality. They were astonished to find that not only was quality enhanced, but there were gains in productivity. What's more, the employees' income rose and costs were reduced, because they were doing things right the first time.

Whether you use an incentive program or a secret checkup system, it is important to have some way to monitor service. Karl Albrecht and Ron Zemke's book *Serving America* is another good source. Search them for ways to improve your service program and attitudes. And don't forget the library. There is more there on service than any of the other Seven Practices of Enduring Businesses. That should tell you something.

The Importance of Quality Is Misunderstood

The purpose of this book is to encourage entrepreneurs. It is not that difficult to start and run a business. It requires mostly elements of common sense and can be achieved by almost anyone who has the desire to do so. For this reason, I want to emphasize how important quality is to success.

You must understand that there is always an entrepreneurial opportunity to cash in on the practice of good service. For years, service has been slipping in American business. *U.S. News and World Report* had a three-page story asking, "Whatever Happened to Service With a Smile?" in their October 15, 1973 issue. *Time* magazine was concerned enough to ask in their February 2, 1987 issue, "Why is Service so Bad?" Report after report can be found that despite rhetoric to the contrary in advertisements and company slogans, professed customer-first policies are not leading to customer satisfaction. Pressure to increase short-term cash flow and profits, among other things, has led to major losses in some industries to foreign markets. It has literally killed some industries.

In *Production* magazine, August 1985 issue, an article was written by James L. Koontz which states, "This lack of service was the single most important contributor to the Japanese success." He was referring to the U.S. machine tool industry.

Thomas R. Horton, president of the American Management Association, in a speech delivered to the Common Wealth Club of California in San Francisco, January 11, 1988, stated the following:

> Salespersons at many department stores appear ignorant of both their merchandise and the rudiments of customer service. Flight attendants often seem more interested in socializing with one another than in attending to their passengers. Bank employees are confused by any but the most simple transactions and seem interested in none. Merchandise ordered by mail arrives in the wrong size or color, and the formidable challenge of getting the order corrected falls to the customer. . . . Sadly, we are not moving toward a service economy, but a no-service economy.

When is business in America going to recognize that they must move toward a service quality policy? Let's hope you can catch the vision early. In the 1960s, the emphasis was on marketing. That was the way to achieve a competitive edge. In the 1970s you heard a lot about manufacturing, the way of the future. The 1980s began the push for quality which has led us to expanding that emphasis to quality customer service here in the 1990s. The lesson to learn from the experience of companies who perform well is that quality service pays. It pays not only by avoiding the drawbacks of poor service, it also pays in hard dollar benefits over the long run by keeping satisfied customers. Remember my insurance company example. They paid my little single-owner business over two million dollars in an eighteen-year period because they were satisfied with the service. In *Total Customer Service*, William H. Davidow and Bro Uttal state that total customer service is the ultimate weapon. They conclude, "In all industries, when competitors are roughly matched, those that stress customer service will win."

Learn from the Japanese

In the late 1940s, the Japanese got some help from some Americans in quality improvement. W. Edwards Deming, Joseph M. Juran, and A. V. Feigenbaum gave Japan some advice on how to improve their economy and improve commerce. Their advice had to do with quality improvement. There is much speculation among scholars on whether they had a major or minor impact on quality improvement in Japanese industry. Some argue that Japan began the quality revolution on their own based on necessity after World War II, the impact of which was felt in the United States beginning in the early 1980s.

Entrepreneurs of the 1990s, beware. Learn the lessons of experience. Learn the lessons of entire economies of powerful free-world nations. People want quality service and products. They demand it. Whether Japan helped America or Americans helped the Japanese, or whether it came out of experience in joint ventures between the two countries, is irrelevant to the lesson learned. It has become a major practice of enduring, successful companies, and it has to be addressed in the 1990s by all who aspire to succeed in business.

In Summary

Quality of services and products, as subjective and personal as it is, is easy to master for anyone going into business. It just takes a little common sense. People want to be treated well, and they want to feel good about their experience with your business. Most of all, they want to come back and use your service again. They don't want to keep trying to find someone that can do it right. Every businessperson should want customers who keep coming back.

Quality, in products and in services, has become more and more competitive. New companies will have to pay attention to the demands of the public in this area. Because quality is in high demand, and because a great majority of companies are still not on board the service ship yet, there are great opportunities. People are always looking for better products and service. Now is the time to join the ranks.

Among the opportunities is clearly the profit that can be made from doing it right the first time. Another opportunity is the enduring clientele created from having a good experience with your company. Even though we have been talking about service since about 1980, American business has been slow to respond. There is plenty of room for newcomers to get their share. New entrepreneurs are likely to find most of their competition still watching what's going on, rather than acting to make it happen.

It's a big job to get large companies to turn around their service competitiveness. It's not easy to teach an elephant to dance. However, for start-up entrepreneurs and other small companies, the necessary ingredients are common sense and a desire to succeed. Seeing to it that your products and services have a reputation for quality may just be what keeps you in business for years to come.

Chapter 9

Practice Six: Don't Embark without a Map

The Practice of Implementing Basic Business Planning from the Start

If you don't know where you are going, you will end up somewhere else.

If you don't plan for the success of your business, you have planned for its failure.

Have a Plan

Everything you do in life, from putting on your clothes to running a business, has a plan. Nothing is ever accomplished without a plan, even though you may not sit down and write it out. You may not even spend one second thinking about some things you do. You just do them by habit and instinct. But there is a plan.

Certain things work well that way. There is no use spending time writing out a plan to put your grey pants on. Just do it the way you always do it, one leg at a time. The plan for such an action is already in your head. You thought about it before you did it, but an exhaustively thought-out, written plan was not necessary.

Why Some People Don't Plan

In counseling experienced as well as prospective entrepreneurs, I find that they tend to want to do everything with the same amount of effort that it takes them to put on their pants: brief thought—reactive and automatic—and no writing. They think that just keeping it in their heads is enough and that they will always be able to remember what they need to about their plans and goals. The truth is, they almost always go away saying they will do it, but never do.

The reason people don't accomplish their goals and plans in business is that they forget them. People do what they are thinking about each day. Many people decide in the morning what they are going to do that day and, without writing it down, do just fine on accomplishing each goal. Others write down everything they will do during the day in their planners. The problem is that the long-term goals, such as beginning a business with its end in mind, get forgotten. If the long-term goals and plans are not in the face of the entrepreneur daily, they don't get acted upon. People do what they are thinking about. That is why almost all the success literature suggests writing out your goals and reading them twice a day. If you don't do that, you get caught up each day in the business of reacting to the day's problems, or managing by crisis. The long-term goals get put off, sometimes forever.

How Plans Help

Business planning is similar to personal planning and goal setting. You won't work toward the goals you have set if you forget about them. Your managers can't help you with your goals if they don't have them to look at and work on. You can't check the progress of company goals and mission statements without a clear understanding of what employees are working on.

The need for a business plan just makes sense, and there aren't many arguments against the practice. Every business must have a format, a written business plan. Yet still a large majority of businesses don't do it. You would be surprised at how many owners say that they have no formal business plan. One of the reasons is that many of them feel that the process is too cumbersome or detailed—it isn't fun. A lot of the literature on the subject makes preparing a business plan too lengthy and too full of information the fledgling entrepreneur isn't really going to use.

Keep It Simple and to the Point

The fact is, a bound, detailed business plan is needed only if it is requested by investors or bank loan officers. (See appendix A.) Even then, many times people put too much together that will never be read. Investors and loan officers at banks only need certain information, and they should be contacted before the business plan is prepared. They will tell you what they want, and you should furnish only what they request. Do what they ask, do it well, compile it in a formally bound book with title and names imprinted on the front, and submit it in a timely manner. It will impress them to know that you have done your homework and done it well.

A business plan that is only going to be used for the entrepreneur to accomplish his start-up plans and work on his goals is a different matter. (See appendix B.) It should contain goals and mission statements along with a schedule for accomplishing the goals, but as long as it is written and read regularly, it could be written on a long piece of toilet paper. Some business plans with mission statements are typed up on a letter-sized piece of paper. Some are handwritten. Remember, the two important points here are that it be in writing and that it be referred to regularly.

Business Plan as a Checklist

Business plans accomplish other important goals. They also help people follow the correct steps for starting their businesses so they don't leave out some important aspect of running a business. Later in this chapter there will be suggested business plans for different situations. Use them as they apply, and consider them to be start-up checklists.

Functions of a Business Plan

A comprehensive, written plan can accomplish many things for you and your business. At a minimum, the plan will help in the following ways:

1. Development. Particularly in start-up situations, the plan can function as a "to do" list. It helps you establish strategic plans, set realistic deadlines, and delegate assignments. It sets deadlines for you.

2. Management planning. The plan forces you to consider the interrelationships between each facet of the business and often becomes the operating bible for the management of your company.

3. Communications. Whether it be your banker, supplier, or outside consultants, owning and operating a business involves letting key people know what you are doing and what your intentions may be in the future.

4. Sales presentation for funding. Many business plans are written for the purpose of raising capital. A good plan must be well researched and documented. It will have realistic financial projections and assumptions which can be substantiated.

Your Road Map

The importance of a detailed, written business plan cannot be overemphasized. It is your road map by which you make some of your most important business decisions. It helps you know where you are, where you want to be, and how to get there. Without an adequate business plan, you risk making many vital decisions based on guesswork and erroneous assumptions.

Most of the experts who advise entrepreneurs say that business planning is the key to successful business ventures. It is a continuous process. It never stops. Business planning requires continuous collection of facts and data, and it forces you to honestly and objectively analyze the important details about your business activity.

A Full and Complete Business Plan for Lenders

The business plan is a written document that clearly defines the goals of the business and outlines the methods for achieving them. A business plan describes what a business does, how it will be done, who has to do it, where it will be done, why it's being done, and when it has to be completed.

Dreams and ambitions are great and important. But what really counts in the business world are results. Therefore it is important to establish realistic goals with a sound methodology for achieving them.

If you are going to submit your plan to a financial institution as a funding document, it needs to be sufficiently detailed and complete, and it must be packaged properly. Keep in mind that there is no set format favored by all lenders. I have never seen two alike. You must take the initiative and use creativity to come up with your own format. After studying the literature at some length, interviewing bankers and venture capitalists, and looking over various business plans, I have come to the conclusion that the following components should be included in the submission to a lender for most business plans:

1. Cover sheet (title page). Include the name of the business, the names of the principals or owners, and the address and telephone numbers of the business.

2. Introduction (statement of purpose). Include a statement of purpose and information about the loan or funding request. This could take the form of a cover letter. Include the loan terms you are requesting, the purpose of the funding, and how you will be using the funds to accomplish your purpose. Include here your mission statement and other nonfinancial goals. (These are covered below.) Regarding your mission statement, refer to Stephen R. Covey's *The Seven Habits of Highly Effective People*, beginning at page 106, and learn it from the guy who coined the phrase.

3. Executive summary. Include a short description of the venture written in an interesting way. This is the first section that the reader will encounter and should include the more important parts of the plan, such as the main marketing steps and the end result. Explain the company's current status, its products or services, and its benefits to customers. This summary is the first thing read, and it is often the last. Make it good enough to entice further reading. Keep it brief (no more than two pages).

4. Table of contents. Make it easy to look up different sections of the plan.

5. Description of the business. Give a general description of the venture, including the type of business, the status of the business (start-up, expansion of a going concern, or a takeover of an existing business), the form of business organization (proprietorship, partnership, or corporation), why the business is going to be profitable, when the

business will or did open, the hours of operation, and whether business is seasonal or not.

6. Business history. If your business is a going concern, include the salient facts that pertain to your request for funds. Indicate any changes in management, ownership, or structure. A history of successes you have experienced in the past should be summarized here.

7. Product or service. Describe what the product or service is in terms of its unique qualities and value to the consumer. Give sales details by product, region, and industry type. Talk about the product life cycle and any seasonal or cyclical details. Is the product patented or copyrighted?

8. Market. Define the target market, its size, your anticipated share of the market, and the growth potential of the market. Use detail such as describing the barriers to your market and whether the market is growing or shrinking.

9. Competition. Identify your five nearest competitors, your advantage over the competitors, the strengths and weaknesses of your competitors, and what you have learned from your competitors' operations.

10. Marketing plan. Summarize your marketing strategy, your sales and distribution plans, your proposed pricing schedule, who you will be advertising and promoting to, and your use of public relations. Will you be marketing your product by wholesale, retail, original equipment manufacturing, or consumer direct? Discuss trade terms to be given and received. Discuss bad debt expense, warranty expense, and reject rates. Talk about how you will be targeting market segments, and what you have budgeted to accomplish the task. Your marketing plan will be of particular interest to lenders. It should be of interest to you also.

11. Research and development. Describe your research and development efforts thus far and what your plan is for the future in this area. Talk about how this is being accomplished and who the key people are. Their resumes should be included. List any external research and development funds and their sources (such as government) with details of amounts and duration.

12. Manufacturing. Include a description of your proposed manufacturing facility, including such detail as size, location, type of building, and whether it will be leased or owned. Identify why it is located properly for this venture. Talk about your production methods

and supply sources. Is the facility located near suppliers? What is the availability of transportation and labor? Will there be any hazardous or toxic waste problems? Project the condition of your fixed assets and their replacement into the next five years.

13. Management. Describe the structure of management, including the board of directors. Include their names and resumes. Include their salaries, employment agreements, stock purchase plans, levels of ownership, and any other considerations. Name any advisors and consultants being considered. Include an organization chart showing lines of authority and responsibility.

14. Personnel. Describe the personnel needs of your business by skills required, salaries or wages, fringe benefits, and anticipated overtime. If the shop will be union organized, discuss how responsive the union is to management. Describe the local labor pool and how it will meet the needs of the company's skill level.

15. Sources and uses of funding. Identify your funding sources, including how much of your personal assets and money you will be contributing, who else will be contributing, and how much you are seeking from this lender. Describe your start-up needs, how much you will require to stay in business while revenues do not cover all your expenses, and how long you expect to need these interim funds. Provide a balance sheet showing the company's financial condition after funding of the various sources.

16. Historical financial data. If you are seeking funds for an ongoing business, provide at least three years of CPA-prepared financial statements, including balance sheets, income statements, and tax returns. Have the CPA also explain how the statements were prepared, such as cash versus accrual method, depreciation method, or bad debt method, as well as the amortization rate used. Give details on the sources of equity, and describe dividend requirements.

17. Revenue and expense projections. Project your anticipated revenues for the next year. Include a monthly breakdown of projected income, expenses, and profits. Explain any assumptions made in compiling these figures, such as expected sales increases, cost of goods sold, and the nature of the expenses (such as sales expense and general and administrative expense). Include any major capital expenditures expected during the projection period. It may be useful to provide three levels of projections: optimistic, expected, and pessimistic.

18. Cash flow statement. Give a detailed monthly breakdown for one year of your expected cash receipts, projected cash disbursements, and the resultant cash flow of your business.

19. Break-even analysis. Calculate the break-even point for your business and give supporting documentation for your calculations. Report the break-even point both in dollars and units of sale.

20. Capital equipment required. List the capital equipment required for the business. Include the cost of the equipment.

21. Milestone schedule. Set up a schedule for accomplishing your business objectives. Include the actual dates for management follow-up.

22. Risk analysis. Potential problems must be identified and uncovered. Risks must be anticipated and controlled. Recommendations can come from outside consultants specializing in these sorts of projections. The temptation in submitting a business plan to a potential funding source is to gloss over the risks in an effort to accentuate the positive. Believe it or not, the business planning experts agree that you should actually do the opposite when preparing a plan for lenders. If negatives aren't dealt with, deals can be broken. Bankers and investors like to see the truth. They are impressed with entrepreneurs who identify potential problems and have plans to overcome them. Don't forget that there are thousands of entrepreneurs submitting plans to lenders and investors. Lenders and investors don't have any problem finding business plans to review. They are a dime a dozen. The investment community wants down-to-earth plans that honestly show the problems and their solutions. They don't like surprises. They are no-nonsense types that like to make money like the rest of us.

23. Appendix. The appendix should include information which is valuable and supportive to the other sections but has not been included elsewhere. This may include names of references and advisers, drawings, legal documents, agreements, personal resumes, personal financial statements, cost of living budgets of the owner, credit reports, letters of reference, job descriptions, letters of intent, copies of leases or contracts, and any other documents relevant to the plan.

Finalize Your Business Plan Document

Get your final document into presentable form before you submit it for review by financial lenders and business assistance experts. It will be their first impression of your company. Whether you have the plan bound professionally like a soft-cover book, or you choose some less formal presentation, it should be perfect, presentable, and professional, with no spelling, grammatical, or typographical errors. It should be written simply and in a straightforward manner. Remember, its purpose is to communicate. It should be as brief as possible while still including all necessary information. It probably shouldn't be any longer than about forty pages. In order to keep it under forty pages, consider submitting the appendix separately. Since planning never stops, the document should be maintained in a format that will be convenient for you to review and update regularly.

Here is what separates the successful business plans from the failures:

1. Attractive appearance
2. Executive summary
3. Table of contents
4. Perfection and professionalism in grammar, spelling, and typing
5. Proper length

Consider Hiring It Out

The entrepreneur is represented by the business plan to lenders and others. It is his or her plan. But an accountant or other professional, someone who is trained in visualizing the whole picture while attending to the relevant details, can provide very valuable assistance here. Accountants are trained to develop budgets and forecasts and have computer programs to assist in planning.

Be sure, however, that the plan is prepared in close association with you and your staff. A plan is not a plan unless it is prepared by the people assigned to follow it and make it successful. Don't just assign out the preparation of a business plan and turn it in directly without being fully familiar with its details. It is your plan. You will be using it for months and years to come. It contains your mission statement and goals which need follow-up. Stay close to it.

Plans Are Goals

Many businesses don't operate with mission statements, goals, or objectives. They don't know when more funds may be required to meet financial demands. They aren't planning for more employees, materials, or machinery to support growth. They don't know when sales may sharply increase, thereby increasing the demand for additional products or services.

Planning formally forces management to consider their projections or goals and when they want to accomplish them. It is a tool used by those who are successful to keep the future constantly in mind. They always seem to have the end in mind. As the plan keeps goals in the minds of management and employees, it serves as an operating tool to manage the business properly.

Plan Changes

No plan is always entirely accurate. Economic times can change literally overnight. Plans have to be changed regularly and incorporated quickly to effect future management decisions. If a company can't quickly change with the competitive environment, it can't survive.

A Non-Lender Business Plan

Like Yogi Berra might have said if I hadn't coined the phrase first, "business planning is business planning," whether it's done for the bank or for yourself. It is still essential, and it is still considered by some to be the most important thing you do in business. It serves the purpose of preparing a road map for the future of your business. It is a checklist. The same list of components must be used in preparing a plan to start a business where funds are not needed from outside sources. Sure, you could leave off the pages and statements meant to inform lenders about what you are doing, but the substantive components must be investigated and written down. You don't have to type it perfectly, and it doesn't have to be bound. It just has to be in a form that you can understand and follow. (See appendix B for an example. A checklist for business start-up is in appendix C.)

A Business Plan Example

I have examined many business plans, and the best one I have seen is included in the appendix. It should give you a good idea of the tone and content of an ideal business plan. (See appendix A.)

In Summary

Some experts have said that the preparation of a business plan is the most important thing a start-up entrepreneur does. Whether you agree or not, there is little writing in this field that discourages the preparation of a business plan. Almost all scholars and business writers alike emphasize the importance of this practice.

Still, many entrepreneurs just ignore the practice. Then, when trouble appears on the horizon, they are not prepared. They are just living for the moment, not preparing for the future, because they have no plan. To write a plan is to begin with the end in mind.

A plan acts as a checklist for new entrepreneurs and as a road map for all businesspeople. If you are not submitting the plan to a lender or an investor, don't worry about the form. Any kind of written plan is better than no plan at all. At the very least, your plan will have a mission statement and goals to work toward.

Whatever you end up doing, taking the advice of this chapter, or following in the ranks of the about eighty percent of all businesspeople who don't write up a formal business plan, understand that *this is one of the practices of enduring businesses.* If you don't plan for the success of your business, you have planned for its failure.

Chapter 10

Practice Seven: Sell, Sell, Sell

The Practice of Having a Constant Strategy for Marketing and Sales

Everyone lives by selling something.

Robert Louis Stevenson

Marketing

No business can sustain itself indefinitely without sales. Companies without a marketing and sales strategy of some sort eventually fade. Sure, there are exceptions, but for the most part this fact is universal in today's free enterprise economy.

The major examples of this are the large, successful fast food restaurant chains, soft drink companies, and other large corporations that are experiencing tremendous success, yet continue to spend enormous amounts on advertising and marketing to improve their image and market share.

Small service companies should take note, especially the one- and two-person companies. If you don't constantly keep in contact with your customers and clients and continually seek out new prospects, you will eventually lose what you have.

Small service firms with only one or two operators (and this includes most businesses) are the most common violators of this important practice. They can get so involved in everyday operations, resting on the laurels of a current brisk business (which often relies on just one or two major clients), that they overlook the importance of generating prospects for future business.

Most people don't like to sell. It's not easy to get yourself motivated to face the public, only to be rejected most of the time. It's easier to stay in the office and count the money. But most people in the business world would tell you that sales and marketing is where it's at. Sell, sell, sell, they will tell you. You must always be selling.

Definition of Marketing and Sales

Marketing is everything a company does, their total system of interacting business activities that distribute products and/or services to the people who want them. It includes the product, planning, pricing, promotion, distribution, sales, advertising, market research, and sales service. It includes making a profit in a competitive environment. It includes personal selling, people-to-people selling. It includes follow-up with customers, prospecting, entertaining, and informing. It includes whatever activities are needed to gain and sustain market share and to continue to grow. The Institute of Marketing says, "Marketing is the management process which identifies, anticipates, and supplies customer requirements efficiently and profitably." It is "the right product, in the right place, at the right price." Even more simply stated, you may have the greatest product or service or idea, but if the customer is neither aware of its existence nor convinced of its value, it will not succeed. You could be the best contractor in town, but you won't get hired if no one knows about you. Marketing, simply put, is how you get the word out and keep it out.

Many of the subjects which make up an integrated marketing strategy have already been addressed in this book. Treating people well and gaining their trust are as important to marketing as they are to personal sales or advertising. Being reliable and dependable will also sell you and your product as well as anything. But no matter how good you are at what you do, how well you have planned, how much trust you have created, how well you treat your customers, or even how much they like you, circumstances beyond your control can cost you their business. Their budget constraints or economic conditions can end it. Or, as many businesses have learned, your service or product can be replaced by your best customer's brother-in-law.

For this reason, sales and an ongoing marketing plan must be continual. In a large company, such a plan is detailed, lengthy, and meticulously followed. In a smaller company it may just be listening to customers, staying close, and constantly searching for prospects. In both cases, and for virtually all companies, marketing is a way to plan for profits geared to the wants and needs of customers. And it often makes up the largest part of a company budget. The average corporate sales and marketing budget is between fifteen and thirty-four percent of the total budget.

Every business organization, from IBM and Federal Express to the neighborhood one-person carpet cleaning company, performs two functions. They produce a product or service, and they market it. As soon as a company drops one of those functions, it is out of business.

A History of Marketing

While marketing was a hugely popular subject in the 1970s, it still has relevance for study today since marketing is customer-oriented. Planning profits based on production needs and studying and emphasizing manufacturing was basically ended by the 1960s. Customers became the focus of the 1970s and service is the hot subject of the 1990s.

Prior to the 1970s, some commentators called the history of business the days of wine and roses. I suppose they would exclude the 1930s, but in any discussion they would have to admit that business is never automatic, nor easy. Consumers are no longer stupid, and marketing means finding out what they want and proceeding to provide it.

In the production-oriented era years ago, the theory was that a good product would sell itself. If that used to be the case, today it is not enough. We have apparently come along way. Today, a marketing effort is necessary to succeed in business. It is not enough for an airline to give good service and get you comfortably from point A to point B. They now must paint their airplanes with bright colors, dress their flight attendants in quality, name-brand uniforms, give incentives to travel agents, spend millions on advertising, and price their flights to attract travelers.

Remember Ford's slogan, "They can have any color they want, as long as it is black." There were more customers than cars, and it should be easy to see why production took precedence over marketing. Today, even the one-person store or service must concentrate on seeking and satisfying customers. It is a buyer's market in most cases today. Products and services must be sold, not just produced.

The literature is clear: technology is changing the way we do business, and consumers are becoming more sophisticated and demanding. The business world is changing. It is not business as usual for the 1990s. We have been given fair warning. We all must adapt to this new marketing era.

The Study of Marketing

This book is not meant to be a lengthy, detailed treatise on marketing. The subject of marketing takes up whole shelves at the library. It is a widely studied and published subject. Students can emphasize this subject in their management studies, and many companies have a director or vice president who devotes all of his or her time to this subject.

What is important to learn is that marketing and sales is one of the important functions of business owners that must be constantly addressed in order to endure. Some functions may survive the temporary back burner, but this function cannot. In sales and marketing, you reap what you sow. If you didn't sow in the spring, you won't reap in the summer.

The Difference between Marketing and Selling

Selling is part of a marketing strategy. It could be explained that the function of sales is to promote and sell the company's product or service, while marketing involves the entire product life cycle in deciding what the customers wants and giving input into the product's development. Marketing, practiced properly, might make selling superfluous, but most people will agree that selling remains an integral part of an overall marketing strategy.

Most large companies spend a significant portion of their budget on an overall marketing strategy with many people involved in executing detailed marketing plans. Smaller businesses may lack this sophistication and often lose the perspective of what an effective marketing mix can produce. It is still very important that small businesses have a marketing plan and operate under a marketing concept. However, to a smaller business marketing may mean maintaining quality business practices and continuing basic sales program.

The other six of the Seven Practices of Enduring Businesses are part of an overall marketing mix. Just doing business daily is marketing. Proper planning, along with treating people well, being reliable, building trust, and maintaining quality are certainly aimed at getting return customers. Practicing such principles of business will help keep customers and will help create new business through referrals from happy customers. But every businessperson must realize that all products and services must be sold—constantly. Markets are never static. While some are more fluid than others, no market goes on forever.

The difference between sales and marketing can be illustrated by an example. A guy stops by a new car dealership and looks at the various cars on the lot. After looking at them and perhaps taking one out for a test drive, he says, "It's beautiful, but I don't really need a new car right now." What he probably means is that his car is still in good condition, it's doing its job, and it could last for many more miles. Getting the guy onto the car lot was a function of marketing, but getting him interested enough to part with his money is a function of sales.

Advice for Large Firms

Only one sentence will be devoted here to marketing advice for large firms. Hire the most highly qualified marketing person you can find who has studied the subject and had lots of experience in large organizations, give him or her a large budget, pay your sales people commissions, and don't be concerned when they start making more money than you.

Advice for Smaller Firms

Most people don't like to sell. As important and lucrative as this field of endeavor is, even sales people will tell you it is not always fun, and if there were an easier way to make it, they would switch. Cold calls, or any calls at all, are just something to procrastinate. There are much more enjoyable functions. Most small business owners would just prefer to see the business come in the door without effort.

Some people have rationalized that selling isn't even necessary. It's too costly, and intelligent consumers will find their product or service one way or another anyway. Well, you don't have to be a brain surgeon to figure out that people won't come to you if you don't tell them where you are. Even the most intelligent consumers need help with certain kinds of knowledge and must be told in some way where to find what they want.

Owners, you don't have to be Super Salesperson if you don't want to. But you have chosen to be a business owner. Since you have made that decision and want to continue successfully, here are some suggestions for a minimum program of marketing and sales that should encourage you.

1. Concentrate on the other six practices. Probably seventy-five percent of your marketing program is performed in concentrating on the other six of the Seven Practices of Enduring Businesses. Be one of those companies that doesn't give customers any reason to go elsewhere. Let the only reason they leave you be because their relative just started the same kind of business. If you are reliable and honest, treat people the way you like to be treated, plan properly, and never compromise on quality, you have performed well on the all-important marketing strategy. With these qualities present, your customers well come back, and word of mouth will continue to feed your customer base. After all, some companies exist forever this way, never advertising and never selling. Quality and service is their marketing program.

If you are satisfied with your growth or level of business using this marketing strategy, then you may want to consider "not fixing what ain't broke." But remember the law of the harvest and the fact that business seldom remains static. That kind of a program works for very few. The better idea is never to rely totally on your service and quality product to produce future business.

2. Sell, sell, sell. Most businesses only exist temporarily without sales. Some owners seem to rest when times are going well, thinking it will never end. Those with success through the years in growing businesses will almost always tell you that the answer is to be selling constantly. Even if you are the owner and salesperson and only have a little time to devote, continue a sales promotion program, no matter how small. Someday you'll be glad you did.

3. Don't put all your eggs in one basket. Many small firms are born and exist because they have that one big customer or client who feeds them most of their business. Trust me, all good things come to an end. Most of those kind of customers eventually go away. What an excellent opportunity to develop other customers while you are riding high. Use their name on your reference list and take the opportunity to build your list of clients while you can. Don't cut back on your program of marketing and sales because you are riding high with that one client. If you have one client that is more than forty or fifty percent of your business, now is the time to be pushing for more business.

4. Get someone to help you. If you just can't stand selling to the point that it doesn't get done, then get other people to help you. Pay them a fair commission for their efforts. Don't be discouraged if they develop the business to the extent that they make more than you do. That happens often. Try not to let it bother you how much they make. Concern yourself only with how much you are making and how the company is growing. Make sure you provide the sales people with what they need to be successful. Above all, see that they have an opportunity, not a job. They'll get tired of it if it's just a job. They will develop your business for you and stay around for a while if it is an opportunity.

5. One a day rule. If you don't like the idea of hiring sales personnel and are relatively happy with the growth of your company, if you want to grow slowly and aren't elated about selling yourself, use what many salespeople use to motivate themselves to do cold calling. Many salespeople who dislike cold calling tell themselves they will make one, or five, or ten cold calls per day. Then they are done. They do it and then it's over. That makes it less painful. Look at it this way. If you make no contacts with customers or prospects, at year's end you will not have made any calls. No promotion will have taken place. No relationships will have developed.

But if you made one sales call per day (most could live with that) by year's end you will have made around two hundred fifty. That amount is substantial, and it accumulates only if you make that one call per day. That is a lot of calls for some small companies, and it could mean good growth. You will have to set the number for your company. It may be two per day. Make the number something you can live with. Make it a number that you won't mind doing each day, something you can keep up with. If it is too big, you won't do it. Consider the number it would be at year's end and force yourself to keep up. You'll be surprised at the results.

6. Attitudes about selling are shifting. Nonprofessional hucksters have tainted the image of the true professional salesperson. Many people don't want to consider sales as a career for that reason. They fear that people will look at them as a huckster. Many owners feel the same way, so they procrastinate the all-important sales function.

But attitudes are shifting and more and more college graduates are headed for sales jobs. High-pressure sales techniques aren't working anymore, and low-key approaches work much better today. Selling requires self-discipline, motivation, and a desire to serve. The job of selling is to influence, persuade, and convince people to purchase your goods or services. It helps humanity, the economy, and your business. If you have a bad taste in your mouth about salespeople and their function, you should attempt to change that image in your mind, proceed to understand the importance of sales, and refrain from using any of the huckster techniques yourself. Be honest and positive, but not pushy. In real estate, the motto is "location, location, location." In business the motto is "sell, sell, sell."

7. Develop relationships. Selling isn't all personal, face-to-face pushing of products and services. Often, selling involves developing relationships that last for years. I spent about fourteen years associating with the CEO of a large corporation, dropping little hints about his company becoming a client and using my service. It finally happened in a big way, and the extended effort paid off. When it happened, some people called me lucky. They didn't know I had been working on it for years, letting him know what I did, and that I would like to be serving his company. When the opportunity was right and the need was there, he hired my firm.

Earlier we discussed that after-sale follow-up means more to clients and customers than many people understand. When you continue to keep in contact with happy clients, you develop word-of-mouth business and future repeat business. If you don't like selling, then take the pressure off yourself and just develop relationships without selling. You'll be surprised how much that technique pays off in sales and how much the practice is really marketing anyway.

8. Advertising. An emphasis on advertising often falsely relieves the obligation for the owner to perform the sales function as frequently.

Advertising is just one more way to communicate your product or service to the public in an impersonal way. It can be an important way to promote. Advertising is obviously not as effective as personal contacts, but it should be considered important in most businesses.

Some companies waste money on advertising. Be sure to test the ads before settling on any one method, and seek to determine if your advertising is sending your message to the right customers. Some businesses should be in the yellow pages, and some should not. Don't waste your money, but be there if you should. Do what is customary and needed in your type of business, and do what works best. Whatever you do, don't substitute advertising for personal selling when your type of business requires personal contacts and sales closings. Advertising may cost much less per contact, but is much less effective in persuading and closing sales to customers.

9. Marketing plan. Like anything else, marketing doesn't happen if it isn't planned. As we have discussed, the achievement of anything is a process that includes a very important step—planning.

Large companies have thick, detailed, written marketing plans that are difficult and time-consuming to prepare and tedious to follow. A small business, especially a one- or two-person company, may not need such a plan, but in order to have an intelligently directed marketing strategy, it must have distinct objectives and a written plan to follow. It may just be notes in a folder for the owner's eyes only, but like any achievement, you will forget the details if it is not written down.

For you corporate people, find a book at the business library that will show you how to do your several-hundred-page plan. For you smaller companies, be sure to include some plans for the following:

    a. Prospects: who are they and how you will go about reaching them.

    b. Competition: who they are, what they are doing that works.

    c. Budget: how much you can spend for all marketing and sales activities.

    d. Strategy: what you will be doing on a regular basis to market, advertise, and sell.

e. Testing: what you will do to find out what works best for promotion, and how well the customer has accepted your product or service.

f. Forecasting: what goals and dates you will set for desired results.

In Summary

The best summary of what marketing really is all about was stated by Herman R. Holty in *The Secrets of Practical Marketing for Small Business*, page 34. He said, "Anything that helps capture a customer's attention, breaks down sales resistance, breaks trail for a salesperson, or gives a customer the slightest additional reason to notice you and become interested in what you offer, is marketing. It is important that you never lose sight of that. Customers are what business is all about, for without them there is no business."

Yes, lack of marketing strategy and planning is one of the best-known reasons for business failure. Businesses that endure know that if you don't constantly get the word out about what you have, people will go somewhere else to find it.

If you have a negative stereotype of sales and marketing people, understand that it is probably a result of your past experiences. It really is a false stereotype and not true of most professional salespeople, especially today. Whatever your opinion of the field of selling or your distaste for selling, realize that it is absolutely necessary to the success of your business and to the free enterprise economy in general. Until something is sold, nothing really happens in such an economy.

Develop a policy of constant sales and an ongoing marketing strategy in your business, no matter how small. Never stop selling, no matter how well you are doing. In sales the lesson equates to the law of the harvest. You reap only what you sow.

Afterword

There seems to be little room for discussion regarding the fact that self-employment, even in a one-person business, is about the only real way to make it in this world. Though many people want the comfort of a job, many more are looking at breaking out on their own these days. There is no question that times are changing in the world of employment. With "right-sizing," more accurately described as "down-sizing," the so-called decade of the entrepreneur may be born out of necessity.

As has been shown, competition, particularly in service businesses, is down because operators think bottom dollar, not commonsense good business and people practices. When competition is down, opportunity is up. By using the commonsense practices outlined in this book, any entrepreneur can and will find success, particularly in a high-demand service business.

There is no end to the resources available to those who need help along the way toward entrepreneurship. The library shelves are full, and the SBA has plenty of resources. Hopefully, this book has taught you valuable lessons, and more importantly, encouraged you. If that is the case—or even if it isn't—we would love to hear your comments. If you need to talk to someone who has done it before, Mr. Astle stands ready to help.

To request Mr. Astle to speak to your group, to find out about his seminars and consulting services, or just to be included on the Entrepreneurial Group's mailing list for books and other materials relating to this subject, write or call:

The Entrepreneurial Group
P.O. Box 803
Provo, Utah 84603-0803A
(801) 226-8266
1-800-868-7777

Appendix A

Business Plan for Submission to Lenders

ABC Sport Shoes, Inc.

A Business Opportunity

Contents

Executive Summary 5
   The Corporation 5
   Objectives and Projections 5
   Management 5
   Market Analysis 6
   Technology 6
   Strategy 7

Market Analysis 10
   Market Overview 10
   Market Characteristics 11
   Competition 11
   Product Categories 12
   Historical Cycles 15
   Opportunities 16
   Market Penetration 16
   Technical Competitive Analysis 17

Product Plans 19
   Product Overview 19
   Current Products 19
   Patents 21
   Development Schedule 22
   Future Directions 22

Marketing Strategy 24
   41 Major U.S. Markets 24
   Product Positioning 26
   Advertising 27
   Promotions 28
   Merchandising 28
   Technical Representative Network 28

Sales Plan 29
  Target Customers 29
  Pricing 29
  Programs 29
  Channels of Distribution 30
  Sales Advantages 30
  Sales Organization 32

Manufacturing 33
  Manufacturing Plan 33
  Facility Requirements 33

Management 34
  Organization 34
  Administration 34
  Sales 35
  Marketing 35
  Finance 36
  Research and Development 36
  Board of Directors 37
  Remuneration of Management 37

4

Executive Summary

The Corporation

ABC Sport Shoes, Inc., a development-stage company, headquartered in Indianapolis, Indiana, was formed to manufacture and distribute high-performance sport shoes. It is the company's intent to become the largest brand athletic footwear manufacturer in the United States by using superior technology and dynamic cosmetics to dominate the technical/primary user side of the industry and secure a major market share by drawing sales from the fashion side. ABC will be a sales- and marketing-driven company that will successfully capitalize on the market shifts towards attractive athletic footwear with a solid technical foundation.

Objectives and Projections

The company's short-term objectives are to raise $5.4 million in new equity financing to be used for working capital, start-up expenses, initial design costs, marketing, manufacturing, and distribution, and to accelerate research and development of new products and designs. This money will come from a private offering coupled with the formation of a joint venture partnership with a Taiwanese shoe manufacturer. The company's longer-term objectives are to produce revenues of $250 million by 1994, with after-tax profitability exceeding 10%. Objective milestones will be followed to determine progress and alert the company to potential problems.

Management

The management team consists of a number of individuals hand-picked for their expertise in certain areas. John R. Harrington, the president, has over fifteen years experience in the industry, most recently as president of All American Marketing, Inc., a sporting goods

5

manufacturer's rep company representing Sport Athletic Footwear. Burton P. Smith, the vice president of sales, has over 23 years experience in the industry as the president of P.G. Sporting Goods and most recently as assistant vice president of All American Marketing, Inc. Robert M. Jones, vice president of marketing, has over 22 years experience in marketing, advertising, and promotions. The vice president of finance, Paul Williams, has six years experience as a cost accountant with Continental Steel. The research and development department will be divided into two areas. The sports performance lab will be headed by Ronald D. Woods, vice president. Mr. Woods adds twelve years experience in sport sciences. The engineering area of the research and development department will be headed by Kirk McDonald, vice president, who has over eight years experience in product design and testing.

In addition, ten middle management personnel have been added for their expertise in specific areas of need.

Market Analysis

The total United States branded athletic footwear market is projected to be $3.4 billion in wholesale sales in 1988, up 10.6% from the 1987 level. Sales volume has increased 64% in the last three years (from $2.1 billion in 1985 to $3.4 billion in 1988). Industry projections are for a minimum 7% growth per year for the next five years.

Technology

ABC will differentiate itself from virtually all competitors in the industry by using a unique, architecturally-structured midsole design rather than the predominant foam padding which compression sets and loses its shock absorbing capacity rapidly. This special technology greatly lessens all shock forces created in athletic performance and thus translates into both superior injury prevention and considerably longer product life expectancy. This technology has patents pending by its inventor in the United States, Canada, Japan and seven European

6

countries.   ABC has a signed letter of intent with the inventor for exclusive use of this technology.

Strategy

The company's strategy for fast growth and market leadership encompasses four principal areas: Technology, Product, Markets, and Sales and Marketing.

Technology.   Six major technology research and development projects are planned or already in progress. They include:

1. Immediate emphasis on incorporating the special midsole design into all seven product categories under development.
2. Testing and patenting a unique air channel insole design.
3. Development, in conjunction with 3M, of a chemical treatment for leather.
4. Development of the upper design to incorporate unique lacing and closure features designed to add stability and comfort.
5. Development of the upper design and midsole to control stability and flexibility.
6. Design of a sports performance laboratory to test our research and development on athletic performance.

Product. The company plans to aggressively penetrate seven product categories initially.   These include basketball, volleyball, aerobics, cross-training, running, walking, and tennis.   These seven product categories account for 80% of the total industry's sales volume.   The addition of children's shoes and cleated shoes as product categories will be looked at seriously in the third and fifth year of this plan. These two categories account for the balance of the industry's sales volume, but are sold on brand name, not on technical merit. The special technology is also adaptable to a variety of non-athletic shoe applications. Licensing agreements with other non-athletic manufacturers will be pursued.

Production will be done offshore. The company will maintain a full-time office overseas to maintain strict adherence to quality control.

7

Markets. The company will concentrate on the technical/primary user segment of the industry. The target age group will be predominantly 15 to 35 years of age, with the exception of the walking category, which is dominated by the 35 to 55 age group. The product categories of basketball, cross-training, running, and tennis are 70% male. Conversely, the categories of aerobics, volleyball, and walking are 70% female.

The company has targeted nine MDAs (major distribution areas) and 32 DAs (distribution areas) in the United States. These 41 population bases account for almost 39% of the U.S. population. The vast majority of advertising, marketing and promotional efforts will be targeted toward these 41 cities.

Price points will be middle to upper end, reflecting the channels of distribution including upscale department stores, athletic footwear specialty stores, sporting goods stores, family shoe stores, and clubs and/or pro shops.

Sales and Marketing. The company will sell products through the use of commissioned independent manufacturer's representatives. Ten geographical areas reflecting traditional rep boundaries have been targeted. In addition to five major chain stores including Foot Locker, Athlete's Foot, Herman's, Oshman's, and Thrifty, the company has targeted three major retailers in each of the 41 MDA/DAs. These accounts have a combined total of over 3,500 outlets. An additional 4,000 independent outlets will be pursued.

Major emphasis will be placed on marketing, advertising and promotion. An in-house advertising agency will direct corporate advertising. Trade journals will be used immediately, with the addition of primary user print media as is deemed beneficial. Co-op advertising support will be given each dealer in the form of line art, scripts and camera-ready ads as well as ad allowances.

Promotional efforts will be targeted at the primary user. Specifically, the key influencer networks of aerobics instructors, basketball and volleyball coaches, and professional athletes in basketball, tennis, and running will be used to reach this market.

Product sell-through will be addressed on three levels. First, targeted key dealers will be allowed to purchase equity share of the company, resulting in a dedicated dealer network. Second, advanced in-store displays, including electronic displays, packaging, point-of-sale, and gift-with-purchase will be developed. Third, retail sales clerks will be taught product knowledge through the use of company technical representatives and will be rewarded financially as an incentive to sell our products. Professional athletes and primary influencers will be used for endorsements and testimonials.

Technical specifications and test results on the products and their enhancement of athletic performance will be published and distributed quarterly to the primary user markets.

In summary, the company will aggressively pursue the primary user market in all seven product categories by targeting the key influencers in 41 national population bases.

Market Analysis

Market Overview

The total United States branded sports shoe market has experienced phenomenal growth in the last three years. There is a renewed interest in good health through diet and exercise in the United States. This cultural revolution has increased the total number of participants in primary user (exercise more than once a week) activities to 60% of the total population (over 136 million people). In addition, a trend towards a more comfortable lifestyle has included active sportswear and athletic-styled shoes in today's fashion look. The result has been a 63% increase in the total size of the market over the last three years, with a projected minimum 35% increase through 1993. In dollar terms, the $3.4 billion market sales volume in 1988 should increase to over $4.76 billion by 1993. This growth is shown in table 1.

Table 1. Total Market Size

Year	Total Wholesale Sales (millions)
1985	$2,086
1986	2,642
1987	3,074
1988	3,400
1993	4,769

10

Market Characteristics

The market can be divided into two general categories: primary user/technical shoes and fashion shoes. The primary user/technical market is currently 30% of the total market, or approximately $1.02 billion.

Primary user shoes are defined as functional/technical shoes worn for their intended purpose at least once per week. Good examples of this include aerobics shoes worn by aerobics instructors and basketball shoes worn by high school and collegiate basketball players.

The primary user market is dominated by two manufacturers: Nike Inc. at approximately $750 million sales projected for 1988 and AVIA Athletic Footwear at approximately $210 million sales. A number of other companies have specific shoes in product categories that are technical shoes but in general are not considered predominately high-tech shoe companies.

Conversely, the fashion side of the industry is much larger in dollar volume, at approximately $2.38 billion sales (70%). The fashion market is characterized by trendy, comfortable shoes in a myriad of designs and colors. Currently, the trend is towards European styling using bright and bold cosmetics. There are 47 manufacturers catering directly to this market, with an additional four manufacturers whose greatest percentage of sales is in this side of the market. The fashion market, because of its trendy nature, is unpredictable. Brand names can become hot overnight and can lose their popularity just as quickly. There is no dominant manufacturer that has shown long-term lasting capability on this side of the market. The major manufacturers on the fashion side include Reebok International at approximately $1 billion, Converse at $250 million, Adidas at $175 million and L.A. Gear at $72 million.

Competition

There are a total of 53 manufacturers who deal in the product categories we are targeting. Sales volumes in 1987 show six companies with sales in excess of $100 million (Reebok—$990 million, Nike—$571 million, Converse—$250 million, Adidas—$175 million, AVIA—$150

11

million and New Balance—$105 million). Eight companies had sales of $64 to $82 million. Seven companies had sales of $23 to $40 million. The other 32 companies had sales of less than $20 million each and combined to produce a total dollar volume of under $150 million.

The dominant manufacturers in the industry with sales volumes in excess of $100 million have succeeded in penetrating a number of product categories. Conversely, the 47 manufacturers with sales volumes under $100 million can be generally categorized as companies concentrating on a market niche in one or two product categories. Examples of this would include running specialty manufacturers, tennis specialty manufacturers, etc. *To achieve our mission statement and subsequent projected sales volumes, it is critical that we be successful in penetrating a number of product categories.*

Product Categories

It is critical that we not become locked into a market niche by product category. No company in recent history in this situation has been able to successfully cross this stereotype boundary to penetrate other product categories. We do not want to be known strictly as a running manufacturer, etc. We must simultaneously penetrate a number of product categories. The targeted categories include basketball, volleyball, aerobics, cross-training, running, walking, tennis, and eventually children's and cleated.

Basketball. Total sales volume in 1988 in basketball shoes is $620 million. Basketball has overtaken tennis as the largest product category. Basketball shoes are currently being worn as fashion shoes as well as primary user shoes. This category will remain strong in both areas and continues to reflect the popularity of the sport. Technical women's shoes are adding to this demand.

Volleyball. Total sales volume in 1988 in volleyball shoes is $25 million. Although this is by for the smallest of the product categories, it is important to us because of the high-tech image and the channels of distribution and dealer networks we address. This is literally a 100% primary user category.

12

There are only four companies currently competing for major market share in this category.   The popularity of volleyball has increased dramatically with the passage of Title IX legislation giving female sports the same opportunities in high school and college as male sports.   The recent success of the U.S. Olympic teams has also spawned an interest in recreational volleyball teams as well.

Aerobics.   Total sales volume in 1988 in aerobics shoes is $526 million.   This is the only category of shoes that is predicted to decline in sales volume.   It is generally accepted that the sport has peaked in popularity.   Cross-training shoes are also stealing market share from the aerobics category as the consumer is reluctant to spend a large amount of money on a shoe as specific as an aerobics shoe.   Also, the fashion trend is beginning to shift away from the hard-core aerobics look.   As is true in running, there is a polarization in this category towards the primary user market only.

Cross-training.   Total sales volume in 1988 in cross-training shoes is $100 million.   Cross-training and walking are the two largest growth categories in the industry.   This multi-sport functional category eliminates the need for the consumer to buy expensive shoes for each specific sport. This category is also displaying high fashion appeal.

Running.   Total sales volume in 1988 in running shoes is $585 million.   This category is experiencing a modest turnaround in sales volume.   While there are few new runners entering the sport, the trend is towards higher-priced styles.   Because of the intense psychology in the sport, this will be the hardest category to penetrate.   The special technology will be a big key in this category.   As price points get higher, the special midsole, with its greater shock absorbency and longer product life expectancy, will give us something different to sell.

Walking.   Total sales volume in 1988 in walking shoes is $450 million.   The walking category is projected to increase twice as fast as the combined athletic footwear average in 1988.   The number of participants in this sport is projected to double over the next three years. This market is dominated by females, particularly those over the age of 35.   Because of its demographic characteristics, this category will focus on slightly different marketing techniques and channels of distribution.

13

Tennis. Total sales volume in 1988 in tennis shoes is $600 million. This category also exhibits moderate growth primarily from women using this look for casual use. This is still the second largest category in the industry.

Children's. Total sales volume in 1988 in children's shoes is $480 million. This category will increase dramatically over the next three to five years as the children of our target market users become users themselves. Children's shoes, however, are not sold on technical merit. Most children's shoes are miniature models of the adult styles, using the same cosmetics, but not the same technology. Parents are reluctant to pay high prices for children's shoes. They are therefore sold primarily on brand name. Until we can establish a brand name, we will not be able to penetrate this category. Therefore, we want to develop this category for introduction in the third or forth year of our business plan.

Cleated. The cleated category involves everything from cycling shoes to soccer, baseball, and football cleats, track spikes, and golf shoes. As is the case with the children's category, these shoes are not based on a great amount of technology and are sold primarily on brand name. We will continue to look at this category but will not introduce products until the forth or fifth year.

14

Table 2. Product Category Analysis

Category	Sales Volume (millions)	Growth Trend
Basketball	$620	Moderate
Volleyball	25	Moderate
Aerobics	526	Moderate
Cross-Training	100	High
Running	585	Flat
Walking	450	High
Tennis	600	Moderate
Children's	480	High
Cleated	N/A	N/A

Historical Cycles

A wider view of the industry shows a general trend towards a five- to seven-year cycle of brand popularity and dominance. A start-up company achieves its peak sales volume in this time frame before beginning to lose market share. Examples of this include Adidas, Puma, Nike, and Reebok. This business cycle occurs for two specific reasons. First, as a company's sales volume increases, its channels of distribution must broaden. Historically, these manufacturers have chosen to include mass merchants and discounters. As the channels of distribution become saturated, these price cutters erode other dealer's profit margins. As this happens, the traditional dealer base begins to search for other suppliers and brands on which they can make better profit margins.

Second, the consumer in the United States is becoming more sophisticated. Brands that do not have technical foundations thrive during a quick fashion trend but lose their popularity just as quickly. The only shoe manufacturer that has shown staying power over an extended period of time is Nike. Nike is perceived in the industry as the company continuously on the leading edge of technology.

In addition, technical/primary user brand shoes can steal market share from the fashion side by taking good quality shoes and making them cosmetically attractive. It is not possible, however, for a fashion shoe company to steal market share from the technical side. To be successful over the long run, we must penetrate the technical side of the market.

Opportunities

There is not a technical manufacturer today ready to challenge for the number one position in sales volume. ABC intends to be that manufacturer.

The market leader in sales volume today is Reebok, a fashion company. A close look at this company shows a 14% decline in domestic sales in their brand in 1987. This decline is forecasted to accelerate in 1988 to an additional 16%. The second largest manufacturer, Nike, is on a cyclical roller coaster ride. New marketing thrusts increase sales volume initially, but this volume begins to wane as the marketing push matures. Swings of $200 million volume in either direction are the result. AVIA, the second largest manufacturer on the technical side, was purchased by Reebok in March of 1987 and is now included under their corporate umbrella. Reebok has positioned AVIA as their technical arm to compete with Nike. AVIA's sales volumes are projected to slow considerably in the next two years. All of the other major growth lines are fashion manufacturers concentrating on specific market niches.

Market Penetration

The company's aggressive marketing, promotion and advertising campaigns should result in an overall market penetration the first year of

16

0.334% or just over one third of 1% of the total market in the product categories we have chosen. The primary user penetration should be 0.98%. The minimum goal is to achieve a 17.5% primary user market share by the end of the sixth business year.

Table 3. Market Penetration Forecast
(all dollar figures in millions)

Year	Total Market	Projected Sales	Total Market Share	Total Primary User Market	Primary User Market Share
1989	$3,400	$10	0.34%	$1,020	0.98%
1990	3,638	30	0.83%	1,091	2.75%
1991	3,893	70	1.80%	1,168	5.99%
1992	4,165	140	3.36%	1,249	11.21%
1993	4,457	210	4.71%	1,337	15.71%
1994	4,769	250	5.24%	1,431	17.47%

Technical Competitive Analysis

While the trend in the industry is to trademark a name for each technical gimmick, there are really only five basic kinds of technology currently in use. The most well known are Nike's air system, Tiger's gel system, and AVIA's cantilever system. A foam system is being used by Reebok and Converse. Virtually all the other manufacturers use varying densities of foam padding of either EVA (ethylene vinyl acetate) or polyurethane.

The company's technology consists of an architecturally structured system of spheres and air cells. Its unique design allows us to manufac-

17

ture our midsole out of different material, giving us complete flexibility to address shock absorption, stability, flexibility, and energy return in each of the product categories. This technology is the only one available that can be altered by product category by changing its component materials to address the unique force and motion problems associated with the different sport activities. This lends itself to a dynamic and forceful sales presentation and a unique marketing campaign.

The special midsole design allows for an infinite amount of combinations to address the four concerns of shock absorption, stability, flexibility, and energy return, not only heel-to-toe but side-to-side, simply by changing the density and component materials.

In addition to the midsole design, ABC is developing its own air channel insole. This insole will help eliminate the heat buildup and associated perspiration, odor, and blister-causing problems common in leather athletic footwear. This insole design can also be made of different materials and as such can aid in the prolonging of product life expectancy. This technology will also be patented.

Major emphasis will be given to both the research and development and sports performance laboratories. New technologies, including sophisticated lacing patterns and structural outsole designs, will be continuously under development. In-house research will be used extensively for product development and as a source of sales and marketing information.

Product Plans

Product Overview

The company's target market is predominately the 15- to 35-year-old primary-user athlete. Of the seven product categories we intend to penetrate, the walking category is currently the fastest growing and therefore will be one of our primary concerns. This category is characterized by a target market of 35- to 55-year-olds. Our product is based on technology and as such will be positioned as high-quality with medium to high price points. The distribution channels chosen will maintain and enhance both the target market, quality, and price points.

The name "ABC Sport Shoes" was chosen specifically to cater to this target market. ABC creates an air of quality and stature necessary to penetrate this target market without being pompous or obsessed with trends. The name suggests selectiveness which will allow for flexibility in differing cosmetics and technology. Yet it is familiar enough to easily gain a believable image.

Corporate colors will encompass product cosmetics, packaging, point-of-sale materials, etc. and will be carefully maintained to enhance the corporate image and the upscale nature of the product. This penchant for detail should translate into a smooth reception in the high-end department stores as well as the major shoe store chains, resulting in market share crossover into the fashion side of the market.

Current Products

The company will introduce shoes in all seven targeted product categories the first year. Initial introductions for spring 1989 will include styles in the five product categories of tennis, running, walking, aerobics, and cross-training. Fall 1989 styles will include the addition of basketball and volleyball. The sales predictions for the number of pairs by style shown in table 4 are based on current industry date. The company will track weekly sales figures and trends to modify these projections

19

according to strengths and weaknesses by product category. A total of 23 styles in 31 colors will be introduced in 1989. In addition, certain models will be changed cosmetically in limited-size runs to be used for promotions through our advisory boards.

The company is projecting sales of approximately 315,000 pairs the first year. The total number of styles and colors has been kept low enough to maintain adequate inventory levels while still maintaining a strong presence to the dealer network. Preliminary plans are to add approximately twelve additional styles in the second year and that many again in subsequent years.

20

Table 4. Current Products

Category	Product Description	Wholesale Price Range	Sales Predictions
Aerobics	Women's Style A	$25–$30	16,455
	Women's Style B	33–38	11,518
	Women's Style C	33–38	4,937
	Women's Style D	35–40	8,561
	Women's Style E	35–40	3,669
	Women's Style F	40–45	8,227
	Subtotal		53,367
Cross-Training	Men's	33–38	8,339
	Women's	33–38	2,085
	Subtotal		10,424
Volley-ball	Women's Style A	25–30	1,911
	Women's Style B	30–35	1,274
	Subtotal		3,185
	Total		66,976

Patents

The company has filed for patent protection on the special midsole technology. Patents are pending in the United States, Canada, Japan, and seven European countries.   In addition to the midsole design, the company intends to seek patent protection for its air channel insole design and lace-locking features when their designs become further advanced.

21

Development Schedule

The special midsole design is currently in the developmental stage. Prototype samples will be completed around August 1, 1988. Product testing of material components and determination of basic technical needs will also be finalized by this time. Product testing and final design work will be completed by October 1, 1988. First generation product will be available to ship to the dealer network by February 1, 1989. Continuing research and development from both the sports performance lab and engineering departments will allow product revision to be done on a constant basis.

Future Directions

The company intends to maintain its focus on the technical/primary user segment of the industry. Research and development will concentrate on improving the four basic elements of shock absorption, stability, flexibility, and energy return. Technical improvements in the outsole design and material composition will be addressed to enhance product life expectancy. The air channel insole, lacing configurations, and upper design will continue to be improved and refined. Feedback from the field advisory staffs will continue to be channeled into the research and development laboratories to keep them current on trends and problems. Portions of the sports performance laboratory will be made available for special promotional events such as major runs, basketball, tennis, and aerobics events. This will continuously show ABC's dedication to the serious athlete.

The special midsole technology is also applicable to a number of non-athletic types of shoes. While it is not the intention of the company to stray from its main focus, serious negotiations for the licensing of this technology to other non-competing manufacturers in other areas of the shoe industry will be sought. Examples include casual comfort lifestyle shoes, geriatric shoes, institutional work shoes including nurses shoes, postal employee shoes, waitress and bartender shoes, etc., and work boots.

The special midsole technology was designed to be used in athletic footwear. With some minor modifications, however, this technology could be used for a variety of shock-absorbing applications. These applications are not limited to the sporting goods industry but could apply to a number of non-related industries. These licensing opportunities will also be addressed as time and manpower allow.

Additional complementary products may also be included if the return on investment is high enough and if they do not detract from the major focus of the company. These products may include a limited apparel line, athletic tote bags, promotional items, and shoe care accessories. Add-on sales to the dealer network, including our exclusive air channel insoles and specialty shoelaces, will also be included.

The additional shoe categories of children's and cleated will remain under development for introduction when appropriate. Continued focus on the golf shoe element of the cleated category will be maintained because of its relatively large product category sales volume and easy adaptability to the special midsole technology.

International distribution will be sought as company growth and product acceptance dictate. Primary focus will be given to the Canadian, European, and Japanese markets. Additionally, the markets in Australia, Asia, and the Middle East will be opened.

Marketing Strategy

41 Major U.S. Markets

The company has identified nine major distribution areas (MDAs) and 32 distribution areas (DAs) in the United States. These 41 population bases account for almost 39% of the population of the United States. The nine MDAs were chosen for their large populations and high visibility as major marketing and sports hubs. The 32 DAs have smaller but significant population bases and are important local marketing and sports hubs. The major focus of the company's marketing strategy and budget will be targeted to these 41 cities. Tables 5 and 6 list these MDA and DA cities.

24

Table 5. Major Distribution Areas (MDAs)

1. Highest population areas
2. Major regional hubs
3. Major marketing and sports hubs—TV, etc.
4. Major airport and/or convention facilities
5. Stable economy
6. High income areas
7. Major educational facilities

MDA City	Area	Population
Los Angeles	Southern California	11,550,000
New York	Northeast	9,259,000
Chicago	Upper Midwest	6,955,000
Detroit	Upper Midwest	4,180,000
Boston	New England	3,663,000
Miami	Southwest	3,440,000
Dallas	Southwest	2,417,000
San Francisco	Northern California	2,197,000
Atlanta	Southwest	1,724,000

Table 6. Distribution Areas (DAs)

1. Smaller but significant population
2. State or regional hubs
3. Major marketing and sports hub
4. Major airports and/or convention facilities
5. Stable economy
6. Relatively high income areas
7. Major educational facilities

DA City	Population	DA City	Population
Houston	2,410,000	Buffalo	1,016,000
Cleveland	1,848,000	Milwaukee	985,000
San Diego	1,862,000	St. Louis	975,000
Washington D.C.	1,749,000	Baltimore	905,000
Tampa	1,720,000	Cincinnati	873,000
Philadelphia	1,688,000	Columbus	869,000
Phoenix	1,599,000	Indianapolis	846,000
Minneapolis	1,587,000	Portland	811,000
New Orleans	1,462,000	Kansas City	766,000
Pittsburgh	1,450,000	Honolulu	763,000
Denver	1,403,000	Louisville	756,000
Seattle	1,270,000	Birmingham	739,000
San Antonio	1,131,000	Rochester	702,000
Memphis	1,064,000	Norfolk	644,000
Hartford	1,051,000	Charlotte	638,000
Salt Lake City	1,018,000	Jacksonville	603,000

Product Positioning

The company's commitment to research and development will produce significant amounts of technical breakthroughs. The special

26

midsole design, air channel insole, and lace-locking features will immediately position the company as a high-tech manufacturer. Attention to detail in the upper design of the shoes, combined with dynamic cosmetics, will further enhance the product line's position in the upper end of the spectrum. The addition of a unique pair of extra shoelaces, money keeper, headband, etc. will also aid in the consumer's perception of greater product value.

Advertising

The company intends to maintain its own in-house advertising agency. This agency will control all corporate image advertising. Initially, this advertising will be focused on industry trade journals and primary user print media. As the dealer network is expanded, the advertising focus will widen to include more general public print media, radio, and television.

The industry norm is to offer dealer co-op advertising of 1% of gross sales. The company intends to increase this amount to 3% of gross sales for the first few years. This will be important because of the company's desire to use some channels of distribution where smaller dealers are not sophisticated and therefore do not attempt co-op advertising. This added financial support will entice this dealer network to advertise the company's products on a much more local basis. An in-house advertising agency will also be more responsive to dealer's needs and can react to special opportunities quickly.

Multi-colored posters of ABC's professional athlete advisory staff will also be an important part of its promotional campaign. The advertising department will also be able to react more quickly and with more creativity to the opportunities involving this professional athlete advisory staff.

Promotions

Primary user and key influencer promotions will be critical to the success of the company's rapid growth expectations. Major emphasis will be placed on primary user promotions by product category. Examples of this include the company's sponsorship of local high school basketball camps, grass roots tennis and aerobics events, etc. The planned professional athlete advisory staffs will also be used extensively in these promotions. The company will also begin immediately to put together primary user advisory staffs, demonstration teams, and an "ABC Athlete" group of key influencers.

Merchandising

In-store merchandising at the dealer level will also be important to aid the sell-through of ABC's line of high-tech footwear. Corporate packaging will include high-tech graphics and will be used for attractive in-store and retail window displays. Development of point-of-sale materials will also include high-tech graphics.

The company also intends to develop a very limited apparel line to supplement the merchandising and sales potentials of its athletic footwear. This will be an important addition as the company penetrates the high-end department store channel of distribution.

Technical Representative Network

Product knowledge at the retail sales clerk level will be accomplished through the development and use of company technical representatives in each of the nine MDAs. It will be the job responsibility of each of these tech reps to teach product knowledge to retail sales clerks and help with all consumer promotional events. These technical representatives will be added when the dealer network has expanded enough to make this financially feasible. Additional technical expertise will be transmitted to the sales clerks thorough the development of technical manuals and electronic in-store displays.

28

Sales Plan

Target Customers

ABC's target customer will be predominantly the 15- to 35-year-old primary user athlete. This age group changes to the 35- to 55-year-old in the walking category where the demographics of the product category are different. Because of its product positioning, the target customer is also more upscale, with a higher amount of discretionary income.

Pricing

Since ABC's product line will include a great amount of technical features, its pricing structure will be on the medium to high end of the pricing spectrum. Average dealer prices will range from $25 to $45. This translates to retail prices from $49.95 to $89.95. This pricing structure will be in line with comparable products from other manufacturers.

Programs

Future booking programs are common in the industry. Programs are based on such things as total number of pairs, total styles and number of product categories purchased. Accounting discounts of 5 to 13% are common. To entice the dealer network to place future booking orders so the company can better project sales trends and inventory needs, ABC will also explore the possibility of dealer freight programs. Freight discounts with major trucking firms who deal with the port of Portland may help in the development of these programs.

29

Channels of Distribution

The company will adhere steadfastly to the five cleanest channels of distribution: high-end department stores, athletic footwear specialty shops, sporting goods stores, family shoe stores, and clubs and pro shops. Because of its high-tech image and design, ABC will not sell to small mail order houses, mass merchants, or discounters. The only exceptions to this will be high-image mail order houses on the level of L.L. Bean. The company can attain its sales objectives and still maintain tight channels of distribution.

Sales Advantages

The company has drawn from the expertise of its management team to define thirteen specific sales advantages ABC has over its competition. The single most important advantage is that *the company intends to include its dealer network in its equity ownership.* Details will be worked out to eventually provide small amounts of non-voting stock ownership to the dealer network based on their level of sales commitment to the company. This eventual stock ownership possibility should be a big key in allowing the salespeople to get a foothold and create a loyal and enthusiastic dealer network.

ABC will maintain clean channels of distribution which will maintain dealer profit margins at a high level. Profit margins will not be forced downward by competition from mass merchants or discounters. Added product value in the form of high technology and the maintenance of a high-tech corporate image will also help the dealer maintain higher than normal profit margins.

The company is also keenly aware that *customer service is a top priority. ABC will strive to maintain a 24- to 48-hour order processing and shipping record.* Dealer trust and loyalty will be earned through the company's customer-service-is-top-priority attitude.

The company is founded on the basis that its *special midsole design technology is more adaptable* to the needs of the seven targeted product categories than the competition *and it is thus superior* in its ability to

30

address the four basic concerns of shock absorption, stability, flexibility, and energy return. Because of its architecturally structured design, the special midsole will also add product life expectancy, which can be used as an additional sales feature.

The company will match existing competitors' *dating policies and discount programs.* In addition, the company will explore the possibility of adding *freight programs* to dealer stocking orders if freight allowances can be obtained from national trucking firms dealing through the port of Portland.

An *expanded co-op advertising allowance* to 3% of gross sales, up from the industry norm of 1%, will allow the company to receive much more local dealer advertising from smaller dealers than would normally occur. This is one of many programs that will immediately put ABC in a favorable position with the independent retailer.

The company will draw on the equity dealer network for market input and direction by *creating a dealer advisory board.* Periodic meetings with key dealers as well as surveys and questionnaires will be used to communicate dealer concerns and learn of market opportunities.

Retail sales clerks will earn incentives for selling the company's product through the use of an employee spiff program. This program will consist of a combination of free product and cash spiffs. Dealer employees will also be allowed to purchase shoes directly from the company at a discount on an employee purchase program.

ABC will maintain an *in-house advertising agency* that will be available to fulfill special dealer advertising needs on a faster basis. Special dealer promotions or opportunities that would normally be missed because of time constraints should be easier to address. The in-house agency will also allow quicker processing of co-op claims and give the company more control over a broader spectrum of image advertising.

Expanded point-of-sale materials and merchandising aids will be supplied to the dealer by ABC's merchandising department. Careful attention to product packaging, colors, and in-store displays will help the dealer sell through the ABC product line.

In addition, the company will periodically provide retail customers with *gift-with-purchase items or special promotions.* These

31

gift-with-purchase items and corporate promotions will be tailored to local markets, major retailers and specific product categories.

The use of a *company tech rep network* will aid the company's dealer network by teaching product knowledge and sales features to the dealer's retail clerks. These tech reps will also be available for consumer shows or special regional promotions.

Finally, as an additional incentive to get the dealer network to invest their energies in ABC's line of footwear, *ABC will give equity dealers advance shipments of new product introductions* as well as *first opportunity to purchase* pre-packaged *close-outs* of discontinued models. Again, both of these opportunities will allow the dealers to maintain above-average profit margins on the ABC product line.

Sales Organization

The company will sell its products through a network of independent commissioned sales representatives. Traditional rep group boundaries have been used to target a total of ten separate rep agencies. The total number of independent salespeople will include approximately 60 people. As ABC's sales volume increases, additional regional sales managers will be hired. Eventually, the company has divided sales territories into four regions. All company employees and independent sales representatives will also share in the company's fortunes by owning small non-voting equity shares.

Manufacturing

Manufacturing Plan

The company's product line will all be manufactured offshore due to its-labor intensive nature. In order to maintain quality control and on-time deliveries as well as to obtain the best possible manufacturing costs, the company will pursue a joint venture partnership with a Taiwanese manufacturer. Taiwan has been chosen because of its high degree of quality control. The company's product designs must be finalized 120 days prior to delivery due to the long lead time necessary for production and shipping. As joint venture partner, the company will be able to place a greater number of purchase orders with smaller quantities, which will give ABC flexibility in determining sales trends and allow us to react to market fluctuations more quickly.

Facility Requirements

The company will maintain an office and distribution/warehouse facility in Portland, Oregon. Flexibility has been incorporated in the design to allow the company to expand its facility rapidly as the expected growth patterns happen. The eventual goal is to have a fully automated warehouse and shipping facility.

The company's research and development and sports performance labs will also be included in the Portland facility.

Management

Organization

The company will need a total of 28 employees the first year. Sixteen of these employees will be involved in upper and middle management and have been hand-picked because of their expertise in specific areas. The remaining twelve employees will be support and clerical staff.

Administration

The founder and president of ABC Sport Shoes, John R. Harrington, has a BS in finance from the University of Southern California, with a minor in marketing. He has over 15 years experience in the sporting goods industry and seven years experience as purchasing agent with A&B Sport & Team Center in San Diego, California; one year's experience as team sales manager at Steve Smith Sporting Goods in Escondido, California; two years experience as an independent manufacturer's agent with Don Martin and Associates of Santa Ana California; and seven years experience as founder and president of All American Marketing, Inc., a California manufacturer's rep agency representing the AVIA line of athletic footwear. Mr. Harrington has an extensive background in banking and finance, including the formulation of profit/loss statements, balance sheets, cash flow projections, source and use of funds statements, employee benefit packages, insurance, and legal contracts.

Mr. Harrington's responsibilities include the overall direction of the company including its goals, milestones, and objectives. He controls all corporate financing including budgets and the procurement of adequate operating funds. He also controls all legal aspects of the company and is directly responsible to the stockholders and directors.

Sales

The vice president of sales, Burton R. Smith, has a BS in education from the University of Indiana. He also has an extensive background in the industry with over 23 years experience as president of PB Sporting Goods in Indianapolis, Indiana, and most recently as assistant vice president of All American Marketing, Inc. He has a solid background in finance as well as over 20 years experience in sales in this industry. His retail knowledge as well as his institutional sales background are invaluable assets.

Mr. Smith's responsibilities include the direction of an independent manufacturer's sales rep network. He is also responsible for the development of all sales programs, policies, dating freight allowance, etc. Additional responsibilities include the maintenance of strict distribution channels and complete interaction with the marketing department.

Marketing

The marketing department will be directed by Mr. Robert M. Jones, vice president of marketing. Mr. Jones' educational background includes a BS in journalism from the University of Utah and a basic certificate from the American Society of Banking. He has five years experience as a marketing officer with the United Bank of Utah; thirteen years in advertising, most recently as senior vice president of Sam Nova Associates, Inc., a Utah ad agency; three years with Sports Fitness Wear as vice president; and three years with the Society of Road Runners as executive director. His background is very strong in all three divisions of our marketing department—advertising, promotions, and merchandising.

Mr. Jones's responsibilities include the direction of the marketing department, including the three divisions of advertising, promotions, and merchandising. He will also oversee the functions of the technical representative program whose job it is to teach product knowledge to the dealer network. Mr. Jones's extensive background in the production of print media, radio, and television will prove invaluable in future years.

35

Finance

All financial responsibilities will be handled by Mr. Paul Williams, vice president of finance. Mr. Williams has a BS in finance from UCLA and an MBA from Harvard University. For the last six years he has worked for Continental Steel as department manager of mill accounting and analysis, overseeing $49 million in inventory. Throughout his tenure at Continental, he has been responsible for such things as payroll, account payable, operations analysis, and cost accounting.

Mr. Williams's responsibilities include control of all financial statements, credit issues, personnel and benefit packages, and SEC- and investor-related items.

Research and Development

Because of the nature of the company's product line, the research and development department will be divided into two areas. The sports performance laboratory will determine functional needs of the product based on research of the anatomical stresses produced in each product category. These needs will then be addressed by the engineering side of the department. The company has determined that the organizational structure of the research and development department should consist of two separate divisions.

The sports performance laboratory will be directed by Mr. Ronald Haller, vice president of research and development—sports performance. Mr. Haller's education includes a BA in history from USC and an MA in sports sciences from the University of Utah. Mr. Haller has also received numerous national awards and citations for his work in the field of sports performance. Some of his recent efforts include consultation of shoe design and performance with AVIA Athletic Footwear, Converse, and Nike. He has also been a consultant with numerous professional athletic teams and organizations, including the Los Angeles Rams (NFL). He has extensive background in sports sciences, training programs, rehabilitation, nutrition, and technical aspects of various sport activities.

Mr. Haller's responsibilities will be to head the design team on the functional aspects of the product. He will also coordinate all field testing

36

and will be responsible for the translation of all technical performance data for use by the sales and marketing departments.

In addition, the engineering and technical areas will be headed by Mr. Wayne Johnson, vice president of research and development—engineering. Mr. Johnson's education includes a BS in engineering from the Illinois Institute of Technology, and he has worked for O.E.A. since his graduation. He has over eight years experience in engineering, testing, and analysis of material components, including a wide variety of foams and shock absorbent materials. He is well versed in laboratory techniques and in organizing and maintaining systematic development procedures.

Mr. Johnson's responsibilities include taking desired anatomical results and structurally designing component parts to fulfill those desired results. His duties include input from conceptual ideas, determination of candidate materials, prototyping, design, and testing.

Board of Directors

The board of directors of ABC Sport Shoes, Inc. will consist of seven members. They include a number of the executive management team of the company: the president, vice president of sales, vice president of marketing, and vice president of finance. Three at-large seats will be filled from the start-up capital investors and/or highly qualified and experienced individuals in the wholesale or retailing industry.

Remuneration of Management

The executive officers of the company and their ages, positions and salaries are shown in table 7.

37

Table 7. Executive Officers—Remuneration

Name	Age	Position	Salary
John R. Harrington	36	President	$65,000
Burton R. Smith	47	Vice President of Sales	50,000
Robert M. Jones	48	Vice President of Marketing	45,000
Paul Williams	34	Vice President of Finance	45,000
Ronald Haller	35	Vice President of R&D—Sports Performance	50,000
Wayne Johnson	30	Vice President of R&D—Engineering	50,000

What to Expect

August to September 1988

- Raise $50,000 seed capital

- Secure manufacturing contract

- Raise $2,000,000 capital

- Finalize designs and field test shoes

October to December 1988

- Secure joint venture contract

- Finalize $1,000,000 bank line of credit

- Relocate to Portland—initial hirings

- Begin initial ad campaign

- Prebook spring orders

Investment Dollars

Today	1991	1992	1993
$1	$15	$43	$68
10,000	150,000	430,000	680,000
50,000	750,000	2,150,000	3,400,000

Every dollar invested today in ABC Inc. could be worth $15.00 in 1991.

Nike

Every dollar invested in Nike Inc. in 1980 is worth $40.00 today and has been worth as much as $56.00.

1980	1988
$1	$40
10,000	400,000
50,000	2,000,000

Information includes one stock split

41

<u>RYKA</u>

Every dollar invested in RYKA in 1987 is worth $2.50 today and has been worth as much as $4.00 in 1991.

<u>1987</u>	<u>1988</u>
$1	$2.50
10,000	25,000
50,000	125,000

<u>250% in one year</u>

This has been accomplished despite the following considerations:

- Corporate net loss of $314,000

- Substandard products

- Substandard distribution

- No prior experience

42

Reebok

Every dollar invested in Reebok International in 1985 is worth $108 today and has been worth as much as $250.

1985	1988
$1	$108
10,000	1,080,000
50,000	5,400,000

Information includes two stock splits

<u>Why Buy ABC?</u>

- Experienced management team

- Dealer equity ownership

- Clean distribution channels

- 48-hour shipping—quality customer service

- Special technology

- Dating discount and freight programs

- Expanded co-op advertising

- Dealer advisory board

- Retail incentives

- In-house advertising agency

- Expanded point-of-sale advertising

- Special promotions

- Tech rep network

44

<u>Top Brand Athletic Footwear Is Hot!</u>

- Renewed interest in good health through diet and exercise

- Expanded market

- Fashion look—not just for athletes

- Continued growth

<u>Who Dominates the Sport Shoe Market?</u>

Reebok	32%
Nike	18%
Converse	8%
Adidas	6%
AVIA	5%
other[1]	31%

---

[1]comprised of 47 different shoe companies with an average market share of less than two percent each.

46

Where ABC Expects to Be

Year	Projected Sales
1989	$7,400,000
1990	27,700,000
1991	75,900,000
1992	137,000,000
1993	203,700,000
1994	235,200,000

47

ABC Sport Shoes, Inc.
Projected Statement of Earnings
Six Years Ending August 31, 1994

	Year ending 8/31/89	Year ending 8/31/90	Year ending 8/31/91	Year ending 8/31/92
SALES	$3,200,000	$16,400,000	$42,800,000	$95,600,000
Returns	35,200	180,400	470,800	1,035,091
Net sales	**3,164,800**	**16,219,600**	**42,329,200**	**94,564,909**
Cost of goods sold:				
Manufacturing	1,760,000	9,020,000	23,540,000	52,580,000
Distribution	193,366	441,242	899,738	1,640,553
Other	60,583	289,752	825,985	2,445,397
Total costs	**2,013,949**	**9,750,994**	**25,265,723**	**56,665,950**
Gross profits	**1,150,851**	**6,468,606**	**17,063,477**	**37,898,959**
SELLING COSTS				
Marketing	1,242,158	3,943,792	7,864,007	15,792,195
Sales	608,330	1,220,561	2,257,102	3,551,209
Commissions	192,000	984,000	2,568,000	5,736,000
Total selling costs	**2,042,488**	**6,148,353**	**12,689,109**	**25,079,404**
GENERAL & ADM				
Admin salaries	65,004	78,535	92,344	100,610
Mgmt info systems	157,206	215,632	302,585	423,080
Finance	382,054	678,617	1,015,878	1,372,059
Research & Devel	309,512	370,664	447,267	530,224
Depreciation	119,576	178,317	237,058	295,799
Amortization	10,000	10,000	10,000	10,000
Bad debts	48,000	246,000	642,000	1,411,500
Total G & A	**1,091,352**	**1,777,765**	**2,747,132**	**4,143,272**
Total expenses	**3,133,840**	**7,926,118**	**15,436,241**	**29,222,676**
Operating earnings	(1,982,989)	(1,457,512)	1,627,236	8,676,283
Interest expense	134,384	467,553	1,153,974	2,301,310
Pretax earnings	(2,117,373)	(1,925,065)	473,262	6,374,973
Provision for tax	0	0	0	953,971
NET EARNINGS	**(2,117,373)**	**(1,925,065)**	**473,262**	**5,421,002**

Year ending 8/31/93	Year ending 8/31/94	Total
$169,200,000	$222,800,000	$550,000,000
1,815,021	2,420,014	5,956,526
167,384,979	**220,379,986**	**544,043,474**
93,060,000	122,540,000	302,500,000
2,328,483	2,784,056	8,287,438
5,053,370	6,573,174	15,248,261
100,441,853	**131,897,230**	**326,035,699**
66,943,126	**88,482,756**	**218,007,775**
23,250,608	26,355,636	78,448,396
4,368,034	8,594,441	20,599,677
10,152,000	13,368,000	33,000,000
37,770,642	**48,318,077**	**132,048,073**
110,294	120,923	567,710
517,743	600,024	2,216,270
1,733,848	3,473,369	8,655,825
603,621	669,126	2,930,414
354,540	413,281	1,598,571
10,000	0	50,000
2,475,000	3,400,000	8,222,500
5,805,046	**8,676,723**	**24,241,290**
43,575,688	**56,994,800**	**156,289,363**
23,367,438	31,487,956	61,718,412
2,850,052	2,141,799	9,049,072
20,517,386	29,346,157	52,669,340
6,975,911	9,977,693	17,907,575
13,541,475	**19,368,464**	**34,761,765**

49

ABC Sport Shoes, Inc.
Projected Statement of Cash Flow
Six Years Ending August 31, 1994

	Year ending 8/31/89	Year ending 8/31/90	Year ending 8/31/91	Year ending 8/31/92
Beginning cash	$0	$100,000	$100,000	$100,000
RECEIPTS:				
Collections	2,531,840	13,608,640	37,107,280	84,117,767
CAPITAL STOCK:				
Terry Hunter	50,000			
Offerings	2,000,000	3,000,000		
Total receipts	**4,581,840**	**16,608,640**	**37,107,280**	**84,117,767**
DISBURSEMENTS:				
Expenses	4,650,775	16,709,290	39,312,269	83,371,645
Income taxes	0	0	0	0
Inventory costs	1,485,000	2,970,000	5,940,000	11,880,000
Fixed assets	633,172	329,000	329,000	329,000
Organization costs	50,000			
Total disbursements	6,818,947	20,008,290	45,581,269	95,580,345
Excess (deficit)	(2,237,107)	(3,399,650)	(8,473,989)	(11,462,578)
Minimum cash	100,000	100,000	100,000	100,000
Short-term borrow	(2,337,107)	(3,499,650)	(8,573,989)	(11,562,578)
Beginning deficit	0	(2,237,107)	(5,636,758)	(14,110,747)
Ending borrow	**(2,337,107)**	**(5,636,758)**	**(14,110,747)**	**(25,573,325)**

50

Year ending 8/31/93	Year ending 8/31/94	Total
$100,000	$100,000	$0
152,820,965	209,780,985	499,967,477
		50,000
		5,000,000
152,820,965	**209,780,985**	**505,017,477**
140,696,035	186,137,973	470,877,687
953,971	6,975,911	7,929,882
8,910,000	5,940,000	37,125,000
329,000	329,000	2,278,172
		50,000
150,889,006	199,382,884	518,260,741
1,931,959	10,398,101	(13,243,264)
100,000	100,000	100,000
1,831,959	10,298,101	(13,843,264)
(25,573,325)	(23,641,366)	0
(23,741,366)	**(13,243,265)**	**(13,843,264)**

51

Appendix B

Informal Business Plan for Use by the Owner

Most writers hesitate to provide examples of personal or business plans. The reason, I suspect, is that they are afraid the plans will be used verbatim. The following business plan is given as an example and should be used as a guide until you have a plan written for your individual business. This type of plan, which is brief and to the point, does not have enough detail to submit it to a lender for a business loan. It does, however, contain much, if not all, of the salient data necessary to guide a small service business. Such a plan, coupled with a more detailed checklist prepared for your particular business, can work well if you read it regularly and change or upgrade it as needed for flexibility.

Business Plan

ABC Carpet & Floor Maintenance Co.

Mission statement. Our mission is to build a floor cleaning service for Tampa Valley that provides excellent, dependable service for a fair price.

Description of the business. The business will be a sole proprietorship, initially providing carpet cleaning to residential and commercial clients. For as long as possible, the owner will work alone to save labor expense. After six months, hard floor cleaning will be added. Plans will be formulated after one year to add general janitorial services if feasible.

Service. We will provide a level of service as described in the book *The Commonsense MBA*, by Richard M. Astle, more specifically described as the Seven Practices of Enduring Businesses. We will gain our natural market share by treating people well, being dependable and punctual at all times, and always being honest so as to build trust. Quality will be foremost in our minds. We will use prudence in our cash management, we will use and update this business plan, and we will constantly market our service, even when business is good.

Market. We will serve Tampa Valley exclusively at first, where over 250,000 people reside. Residential and commercial clients will be sought.

Competition. There are thirteen other such services now operating in the valley. Based on the fact that most are not performing well (the 80/20 Principle of Business), and that most clients are looking for a better carpet cleaning service, we will proceed to obtain our market share.

Marketing Plan

December 1993:

1. Gather a list of potential commercial clients from the owner's father and his partner.
2. Visit Mr. Stevenson for names he promised to give.
3. Get a list of neighbors and friends from the owner's parents for residential clients.
4. Prepare business cards and brochures by January 1, 1994.

January - March, 1994:

1. Begin sales contacts directly to potential clients on the potential commercial list.
2. Hand out one-page brochure to all residences on the residential list.
3. Continue to develop client list.
4. Two sales contacts will be made each day as a matter of practice, no matter how busy we get, or how good business is.
5. Use little brothers and sisters to deliver brochures to doors of residential referrals. Two hundred brochures will be delivered each week.
6. Each customer will be asked for referrals, and the names will added to the continuing referral list for contacts.

Sources and Uses of Funds

Initially, $4,000 will be borrowed from family sources. It will be used as follows:

Carpet cleaning machine	$2,200
Initial supplies (cleaning)	600
Printing (cards, brochures, invoices, etc.)	375
Insurance (first year premium)	450
Office supplies	200
Miscellaneous	175
Total	4,000

Revenue and Expense Projections

Revenues 1994 (goals):

January	$300
February	500
March	600
April	700
May	900
June	1,300
July	1,500
August	1,800
September	2,100
October	2,400
November	2,800
December	3,300
Total	18,200

Expenses 1994 (projected):

Advertising	$1,000
Automobile	3,000
Machine depreciation	3,300
Supplies (cleaning)	3,000
Supplies (office)	200
Postage	250
Printing	675
Total	11,425

Net income (projected)	6,775

Appendix C

Business Start-up Checklist

Introduction

In a pamphlet called *Checklist for Going Into Business* put out by the Small Business Administration and written by members of the Service Corps of Retired Executives (SCORE), it says, "There is a gap between your dream [of owning a business] and reality that can only be filled with careful planning."

As you will see, I am not fond of business start-up checklists as they relate to self-analysis, personal circumstances, skills, experience, and education. Checklists often discourage people as they assist in determining whether an idea is feasible and marketable. Guts and common sense may be better determinants. But a checklist can act as a guide to help you prepare a comprehensive business plan. And it can help you keep organized while in the start-up phase of your business.

Read on and determine what help you want from checklists. Do your own thinking, make your own decisions, and remember that just because an item is on a checklist doesn't mean it necessarily pertains to you or your situation.

Self-Analysis

Checklists that are academically prepared for textbooks or government pamphlets often discourage rather then encourage entrepreneurs. They can be helpful in many areas of planning, but they can also cause unnecessary fear by suggesting that a person may not be prepared enough or that an idea may not be marketable.

When a desire is present in a person's mind, that person is capable of accomplishing the desire or goal. Self-analysis sections of checklists go beyond what checklists should do, and they go well beyond the qualifications of those who usually write them. Questions such as "Are you a leader?" or "Do you like people?" or "Can you work well with others?" simply scare people off who may be perfectly capable human beings with loads of common sense and all the desire needed to be perfectly successful in a business of their own. I say let's keep the psychology and self-analysis out of checklists and keep them objective. What we need is more encouragement.

If you have a strong desire to be independent, to experience the American dream and operate a business of your own, if you are willing to follow the other steps on the checklist and to practice commonsense business principles addressed in this book, you are qualified and ready to proceed. Analyze yourself, and let the scholars and checklist writers analyze themselves. Skip the psychological self-analysis section of any checklist you may see and go onto the next item.

Is Your Idea Feasible?

It is clear that products or ideas must satisfy needs. There are bad ideas that shouldn't be pursued. But checklists often discourage people by leading the reader to think his or her product or service may not fit in the market because of demand or competition. Some even encourage the entrepreneur only to have an original idea, something no one else is doing or has, with no competition.

If you have read this book, you will understand that the 80/20 Principle of Business means that you can start a business in any area with any amount of competition. Any idea for a business can potentially compete, no matter how many others are doing it. Market share can be obtained simply by improving quality and service. Remember, your idea is feasible if there is a high demand and you are willing to compete in a better way. In some businesses, anytime is the right time. For others, do what is necessary to check feasibility by getting advice. Don't skip the "feasible" question. Your product or service must be feasible. But listen to your own head. Make your own decisions. Don't be discouraged just because the checklist says there should be no competition.

Personal Skills and Experience

Most people possess enough skills to constitute the basis for some services, and even to produce some products. Checklists seem to encourage entrepreneurs to have experience as a manager or supervisor and to have experience in the sort of business they are going to start.

That direction is good. But it is not a prerequisite for success in business. It isn't likely that anyone has all the skills and experience needed anyway. You will need to hire personnel to help fill the gaps. But common sense and a little knowledge of how to treat people and how to get people to perform for you will likely fill this bill. Don't get scared because a checklist says you should have extensive business training in school. You can find out what you need to know on your own, and common sense will get you by.

All the education you can get will help. All the experience you can get will help. If you are young and single, I suggest that you finish school. Get as much education and experience as you can. Some people may even want to work for someone else for a while just for the learning experience. That's fine. Just don't ever abandon your dream of self-employment in the process.

Protecting Your Idea

If needed, you may want to apply for trademarks, patents, and copyrights. Usually, a little advice from an attorney who specializes in this area is wise. Many times people make such applications when they may not be necessary. And there are some good books on the subject if you feel inclined to make the decision and the fill out the application yourself. Check your local library. Here is some basic information.

Trademarks. Trademarks are names or symbols used in any commerce that is subject to regulation by state government or the United States Congress. Check with your state for their rules and applications. At the federal level, contact the United States Commissioner of Patents or Trademarks, Washington, D.C. 20231, (703) 557-5168, or call the Trademark Information Hotline at (703) 557-3080.

Patents. A United States patent protects new and useful inventions. Only attorneys and agents registered with the United States Patent Office may represent inventors in related matters. Patents are issued by the Commissioner of Patents and Trademarks, Washington, D.C. 20231. Their information line telephone is (703) 557-5168. Additional information is provided in the publication *General Information Concerning*

Patents and other publications distributed through the United States Patent and Trademark Office. Contact the United States Government Printing Office, Washington, D.C. 20402, (202) 783-3238.

Copyrights. Thoughts and ideas of authors, composers, and artists are protected by copyrights. It prevents illegal copying of written matter, works of art, or computer programs. Contact the United States Copyright Office, United States Library of Congress, James Madison Memorial Building, Washington, D.C. 20540. Their order line is (202) 707-9100, and their information line is (202) 479-0700.

Market Analysis

For some businesses, all that is needed is a knowledge that there is a demand for the service or product and that you have the common sense to practice the seven principles discussed in this book.

In many businesses, however, it is important for the owner to know the market. Before start-up, research that takes time and effort must be accomplished. It can be done by anyone and does not have to be costly. You must determine facts about customers and demand. The more information you have, the better equipped you will be to capture the intended segment of the market. See chapter 10 for details of a marketing plan.

A Written Business Plan

This step is almost mandatory. Much has already been said about this important step. While all businesses have a plan, at least in their owners' minds, only a few succeed without putting it in writing. The importance of writing cannot be overemphasized. See chapter 9.

Legal Aspects

Consider the following important legal steps that will keep you out of trouble and happily in a business of your own:

1. Legal structure. What legal structure have you chosen—sole proprietorship, partnership, or corporation? A few states have adopted the limited liability company as law. A business attorney can give you the best advice for your business, and filing the necessary documents is usually easy.

2. Accounting. How will you keep your books? An accountant should give this advice, but often a simple set of books can easily be kept by someone in your business on a daily basis, leaving the year-end financial statements and tax preparation for the CPA. Operate on a cash basis if possible.

3. Licenses and permits. Check with your local and state governmental agencies to be sure you comply with all licensing and zoning codes and that you have the proper permits. It pays to be in compliance. Do it right from the start. Many businesses try to circumvent these rules, but it almost never pays.

4. OSHA. Will you need to be concerned with Occupational Safety and Health requirements?

5. Worker's compensation. If you have employees, you will need to check worker's compensation laws to be sure you comply.

Insurance and Security

It is becoming increasingly important that attention be given to security and insurance protection for your business. Contact several insurance agents for information on rates and needed coverage. Be sure to shop around, since rates can vary widely. Seek backup advice from your attorney to be sure you are not over- or under-protecting yourself from liability.

Finances

As discussed previously, try to finance your business yourself. Grow slowly if necessary. Loans have to be paid back. Some businesses need almost no funds to start up. But undercapitalization is a reason for some business failures. Some think it is the main reason. If you have a good idea and need financing, don't give up until you find it. There are many good sources of capitalization funding at the local, state, and federal levels. And don't forget the most popular source—your family and friends. See chapter 7.

Get Help

Everybody can't know everything. Attorneys can help with legal questions and accountants can help with tax and accounting matters. They are not the best source, however, for advice on whether to proceed and how. You may need outside help for business questions. There are private consultants, but they are often expensive.

Every state, and many cities, have sources for advice and consultation. Local Chambers of Commerce can be helpful with seminars and other sources.

Probably the best source of help for prospective small business entrepreneurs to receive free, confidential consultation, along with inexpensive literature and quality, low-cost workshops, is SCORE, the Service Corps of Retired Executives. It is made up of mostly retired and some active executives. They provide brains, ideas, know-how and experience—coupled with a desire and ability to share these critical items.

SCORE is a nonprofit organization whose sponsor is the Small Business Administration. There are over eleven thousand volunteer counselors in over four hundred chapters located in all fifty states. They give free counseling and hold regular workshops where experts in all fields volunteer to help train anyone who desires to attend.

Consult your telephone directory under United States Government for your local Small Business Administration office, or call the Small Business Answer Desk at 1-800-368-5855, for information on any of the Small Business Administration resources.

Bibliography

Albrecht, Karl. 1988. *At America's Service.* Warner Books.

———, and Ron Zemke. 1985. *Service America.* Warner Books.

Baida, Peter. 1990. *Poor Richard's Legacy.* William Morrow and Company.

Boone, Loise E. and David C. Kurtz. 1977. *Foundations of Marketing.* The Dryden Press.

Bayless, Jon. 1989. "Starting Your Own Business." *Design News.* June, 146.

Bernstein, Sid. 1990. "Education that Serves All." *Advertising Age.* 27 September, 34.

Bhote, Keki R. 1991. *World-Class Quality.* Amacom.

Boyett, Joseph H. and Fran Tarkenton. 1991. *The Competitive Edge.* Plume.

Braham, Jim. 1989. "The Fear of Success." *Industry Week.* 1 May, 23.

Carpenter, Philip. 1992. "Bridging the Gap between Marketing and Sales." *Sales and Marketing Management.* March, 29.

Cirtin, Arnold and Donald F. Kurtako. "Developing a Business Plan for Your Clients." *The National Public Accountant.* 24.

Clouse, Van G. H. 1990. "A Controlled Experiment Relating Entrepreneurial Education to Students' Start-up Decisions." *Journal of Small Business Management.* April, 45.

Covey, Stephen R. 1989. *Principle-Centered Leadership.* Executive Excellence.

———. 1989. *The Seven Habits of Highly Effective People.* Simon and Schuster.

Crawford-Mason, Clare and Lloyd Dobyns. 1991. *Quality or Else.* Houghton Mifflin Company.

Crosby, Philip B. 1979. *Quality Is Free.* McGraw-Hill.

———. 1984. *Quality without Tears.* McGraw-Hill.

Cundiff, Edward W. 1985. *Fundamentals of Modern Marketing.* Prentice-Hall.

Cyr, Donald G. and Douglas A Gray. 1987. *Marketing Your Product.* Self-Counsel Press.

Davidow, William H. and Bro Uttal. 1989. *Total Customer Service.* Harper Perennial.

Davidson, Jeffrey P. 1989. *The Marketing Sourcebook for Small Business.* John Wiley and Sons.

Davidson, D. Kirk. 1990. "On Corporate Reputation: A Reply to Dobson." *Business and Society.* Spring, 39.

Dunckel, Jacqueline. 1989. *Good Ethics Good Business.* Self-Counsel Press.

Elam, Houston G. and Norton Paley. 1992. *Marketing for Nonmarketers.* Amacom.

Eliason, Carol. *The Business Plan for Homebased Business.* U.S. Small Business Administration Business Development Publication MP15.

Frernald, Lloyd W., Jr. and George T. Soloman. 1991. "Trends in Small Business Management and Entrepreneurship Education in the United States." *Entrepreneurship Theory and Practice.* Spring, 25.

Gerber, Michael E. 1986. *The E-Myth.* Harper Business.

Goldberg, Beverly and Frank Sonnenberg. 1992. "Business Integrity: An Oxymoron?" *Industry Week.* 6 April, 33.

Hagy, James R. 1991. "Hung Upon the Way Up." *Florida Trend.* December, 51.

Hardy, Kenneth G. 1992. "Marketing Competencies for Every Manager." *Business Quarterly.* Winter, 251.

Hartley, Robert F. 1989. *Sales Management.* Merrill Publishing Company.

Haynes, Max and Peter Robinson. 1991. "Entrepreneurship Education in America's Major Universities." *Entrepreneurship Theory and Practice.* Spring, 41.

Hill, Napoleon. 1960. *Think and Grow Rich.* Combined Registry Company.

Holtz, Hermon R. 1982. *The Secrets of Practical Marketing for Small Business.* Prentice-Hall.

Hyatt, Carole. 1990. *Shifting Gears.* Fireside.

Kiam, Victor. 1986. *Going for It.* William Morrow and Company.

Kossen, Stan. 1982. *Creative Selling Today.* Harper and Row.

Lannon, Lynn. 1990. "Giving Back: The Secret of Creating Success." *Training and Development Journal.* April, 58.

Leepson, Marc. 1988. "Building a Business: A Matter of Course." *Nation's Business.* April, 42.

Longenecker, Justin G., Joseph A. McKinney and Carlos W. Moore. 1989. "Ethics in Small Business." *Journal of Small Business Management.* January, 27.

Luther, William M. 1991. *The Start-up Business Plan.* Prentice-Hall.

Maital, Shlomo. 1991. "When You Absolutely, Positively Have to Give Better Service." *Across the Board.* March, 8.

McCormack, Mark H. 1984. *What They Don't Teach You at Harvard Business School.* Bantam Books.

———. 1989. *What They Still Don't Teach You at Harvard Business School.* Bantam Books.

McKenna, Regis. 1991. *Relationship Marketing.* Addison-Wesley.

Moody, Robert W. and James R. Young. 1978. *Personal Selling: Function, Theory and Practice.* The Dryden Press.

Murphy, John A. 1987. *Quality in Practice.* Gill and Macmillan.

Murphy, John F. *Sound Cash Management and Borrowing.* U.S. Small Business Administration Development Publication FM9.

Pearson, Michael A., Cynthia C. Ryans and John K. Ryans, Jr. 1989. "The Adequacy of Coverage in Small Business Courses at American Colleges and Universities." *The Mid-Atlantic Journal of Business* 25 (April):39.

Peters, Diane McFerrin and Hal F. Rosenbluth. 1992. *The Customer Comes Second.* William Morrow and Company.

Peters, Tom J. and Robert H. Waterman, Jr. 1982. *In Search of Excellence.* Harper and Row.

Policastro, Michael L. *Introduction to Strategic Planning.* U.S. Small Business Administration Business Planning Series.

Stabl, Ronald A. 1991. "Trust Is Best Bet for the Mature Market." *Bank Marketing.* October, 30.

Shinn, George. 1982. *Introduction to Professional Selling.* McGraw-Hill.

Sonnenberg, Frank. K. 1990. "A Vision for the 1990s." *The Journal of Business Strategy.* September/October, 52.

Touby, Laurel Allison. 1991. "Eight Lessons from the Bad Times for the Good Times." *Working Women.* December, 40

Tuller, Lawrence W. 1991. *Recession-Proof Your Business.* Bob Adams, Inc.

U.S. Small Business Administration. 1988. *Handbook of Small Business Data.* Office of Advocacy.

——. 1989. *The State of Small Business: A Report of the President.* U.S. Small Business Administration.

Walker, Denis. 1990. *Customer First.* Gower.

Wright, N. Dale. 1988. *Papers on Ethics of Administration.* Brigham Young University.

Yager, Jan. 1991. *Business Protocol.* John Wiley and Sons.

Index

80/20 Principle of Business
17, 21

accounting 239
act now 64
action 55
advertising 170
Albrecht, Karl 147
always call 81
America's record 141
American dream 17, 29
asset, our employees are our
greatest 31, 71
attitude 74
about selling 170

banks 113
belief 45
big companies, what they do
139
blueprint 52
bootstrapping 111
boredom 57
Bowie, Norman E. 102
business image 123
business plan 238
for lenders 154, 175
for non-lenders 160, 229
functions of 153
business planning 151

call ahead 89
caveat emptor 69
caveat venditor 70
character 91
character ethic 91, 95

choices 29, 37
code of ethics 103
cold calls 167
communications 154
company cars 120
Coolidge, Calvin 58
courage 63
Covey, Stephen R. 51, 94
criticism 63
customer service 131

Davidow, William H. 148
deadlines, meet your 85
debt
get out of 126
short-term vs. long-term
116
stay out of 126
decision 50
Declaration of Independence
30
demand 26
Deming, W. Edwards 149
dependable 79
desire 42
determination 58
development 154
dishonesty 92
do it well 131
Dunckel, Jacqueline 102

economy 26, 107
Edison, Thomas 59
education 26, 58
empathy 75, 78
encouragement 17

Entrepreneurial Quotient 34
entrepreneurial skills 34
entrepreneurship education
        33
    in college 32
equity 57
equity lenders 113
ethics 102
experience 26, 236

factoring 115
fairness 78
faith, three sources of 46
fake it 118, 129
fallacies, common 110
family budget 125
fear 62
Federal Express 139, 141
Feigenbaum, A. V. 149
finances 239
    personal and business
        107
    personal and family 124
Five Practices of Prudent
        Family Finances 125
follow up 89
Franklin, Benjamin 107
free lunch 57
freedom 30
funded, fully 110
funding sources 112

gearshift metaphor 40
genius 58
Gillette 111
goal setting 152
goals, long-term 53
Golden Rule 69

government statistics 24
grass is always greener 122

happiness 30
Heinz 111, 119
Hewlett-Packard 111, 119
Hill, Napoleon 61, 62
Holty, Herman R. 172
honesty 86, 91
Horton, Thomas R. 148
human nature 83

ideas 55
Institute of Marketing 164
insurance 127, 239
integrity 91
interview 88
investigation 46

Japan 88
Jefferson, Thomas 29
Juran, Joseph M. 149

keep it simple 153
Koontz, James L. 148

late people 87
leadership, authoritarian 72
leasing, auto 120
legal structure 239
leveraging 117
licenses and permits 239
loans
    government assistance
        114
    personal source 115
    Small Business Adminis-
        tration 114

luck 59

management planning 154
Marden, Orison Swett 91
market analysis 238
marketing, history of 165
marketing and sales
    definition of 164
    difference between 166
    strategy for 163
marketing plan 171
Markham, Edwin 69
McDonald's 109
milestone schedule 54
mission statement 104
money mismanagement 125
mortgage 126
Murphy's Law 87

natural law 45
needs before wants 107
negative 47.
NuSkin 113

one a day rule 169
operate lean
    on assets 121
    on personnel 119
operating debt-free 117
OPM (Other People's Money)
    117
OSHA 239
outside services 119
overhead 112

perform well 64
Perot, Ross 144
persistence 57, 58

personal achievement meta-
    phor 39
personal organization 39
personal success 39
Peters, Diane McFerrin 147
Peters, Thomas J. 96
plan 51
planning 152
    three principles of 54
positive 64
price-sensitive 140
pricing 140
principle 17
priorities 53, 54, 58
priority management 85
process 39, 59
profit-seeking paradox 102
protecting your idea 237
prudence 107
punctual 79
punctuality 86

quality 131
quality product 136
quality service 131, 135, 138
    how initiated 143

Reich, Robert B. 69
relationships 170
reputation 81
restraint 107
review 54
right-sizing 33
risk avoiders 63
Rosenbluth, Hal F. 75, 147

sales presentation for funding
    154
savings account 128

say no 82
scheduling 80
Sears 98
self-analysis 36, 235
self-determination 30
self-discipline 127
self-restraint 127
self-visualization 48
sell, sell, sell 163
service business 21, 60, 76,
        145
Service Corps of Retired Ex-
        ecutives (SCORE)
        235
Seven Practices of Enduring
        Businesses 67
small business 24
Small Business Administra-
        tion 114, 235
South America 88
start-up 109
start-up business 25
start-up checklist 235
Stevenson, Robert Louis 163
success
        a process 59
        defined 41

talent 58
Tarkenton, Fran 131, 144
time management 58
tough times, survival in 109
trust 91
try it 49

undercapitalization 123
United Parcel Service 111,
        119

Uttal, Bro 148

value-driven 96
visualize 47

Waterman, Robert H., Jr. 96
win-win 74
word of mouth 86
WordPerfect 113
work 56
work ethic 31
worker's compensation 239
working smart 56, 58

Yager, Jan 79

Zemke, Ron 147